Going Hard after God

Geary Reid

ISBN: 978-976-8305-39-8

Acknowledgments

Great thanks must be expressed to the following people:

The heavenly Father, for granting me the wisdom and inspiration to record the information in this book, which I began on May 8, 2021, and completed on May 15 2021; my family, for their continued encouragement and support regarding various challenges; and several people who have assisted with reviewing and editing the book:

- Wonnette Nicholson, Dipl. in Business Management and Administration
- Krysta Newton, LL.B, LEC

To you, the reader: have fun while reading, and grasp and practice what you learn so that this world will become a better place. Many people are depending on your guidance. We all need a shoulder to lean on and a hand to guide us.

Rev. Geary Reid
MBA, FCCA, FAAPM, MPM, CAT

Reid's Learning Institute and Business Consultancy

reidnlearn.com

Amazon: amazon.com/author/gearyreid

Facebook: Reid n Learn

Instagram: Reid n Learn

LinkedIn: Reid's Learning Institute
and Business Consultancy

199 Kuru - Kururu, Soesdyke Linden Highway
Guyana, South America

Table of Contents

Introduction

The work of the Lord cannot be done by lazy persons. God needs more persons to follow him all the way, so he is looking for persons who have a willing heart and want to go hard after him. Lukewarmness will not allow believers to have a breakthrough in their lives.

For anyone to work for the Lord, they must first be called by him. Some persons are called by God, but they are trying to hide. It must be known that no one can hide from God, since he is omniscient and watches over the entire universe. When a person comes to the Lord, they must be willing to deny themselves of some things in order to follow him.

Seeking God and his power must not be done haphazardly; it must be intentional. Therefore, persons need to seek God first and not last. God must be everyone's first priority. For those who seek God first, he will do many good things for them. Cling to God now and let him become a blessing to your life.

All believers, whether young or old, must equip themselves with the Word of God and prayer. These are two powerful resources that will give believers victories and allow them to overcome the adversary. Jesus knew the Word and was in prayer, so when Satan attacked him in the wilderness, he responded appropriately to Satan. The Word of God is a lamp and light to every believer's feet, and they must use it daily as they move from location to location. When believers pray, they have the power to bind and loose things on the earth and in heaven, so believers must be fervent with their prayer and see great results.

When persons sin, they must not be ashamed to seek forgiveness from God. David was a great example of a man who sinned and, despite his status, sought forgiveness for his sins. God forgave him and used him greatly.

Persons will become sick. However, good friends must be willing to help those who are sick to be healed. Some good friends are willing to do whatever it takes to help their friends to receive God's healing.

Those who work for God must expect persecution. However, as they work for God, he will deliver them, just as he did for Paul and Silas. No prison is too strong that God cannot break it and set his children free as they work diligently for him.

The Holy Spirit is free and available to all believers. Those who go hard after God need the Holy Spirit in their lives. With the Holy Spirit, they have power as never before. There are many spiritual gifts that are accessible through the Holy Spirit. All believers must allow the Holy Spirit to operate in their lives as they go hard after God.

Those who want to become efficient in their ministry always need a quality mentor. Therefore, every believer must choose someone who will help them to become efficient.

1. Has God called you?

Many persons want to work for the Lord, and they want God to bless them. However, some persons are not sure if God has called them.

It is important for everyone who wants to go hard after God to know if God has called them. When a person knows that God has called them, they will have confidence in following him and his word.

God desires that everyone come after him. Many of the things the Lord wants to do will be done to those who are called to serve him. The Lord has called and continues to call for everyone to follow him.

Matthew 11:28-29

28 Come unto me, all ye that labour and are heavy laden, and I will give you rest. 29 Take my yoke upon you, and learn of me; for I am meek and lowly in heart: and ye shall find rest unto your souls.

In these verses, Jesus made a call for persons who are tired of living in sin to follow him. Everyone who is living in sin has a heavy burden to carry, and this burden will prevent them from inheriting the blessings of God. So, Jesus chooses to call all sinners and to give them hope for a great future.

1.1 Jesus was deliberate in calling sinners

No believer must become angry when sinners accept the Lord. Whenever sinners come to know the Lord, they will not be reducing the blessings which the Lord has for his children. In some families whose income is small, there are often concerns about every new person who is added to the family, since the same limited resources have to be distributed among more persons. However, God has many blessings for everyone. He wants sinners to experience his blessings, and so he has called the sinners and not the righteous.

Luke 5:27-32

27 And after these things he went forth, and saw a publican, named Levi, sitting at the receipt of custom: and he said unto him, Follow me. 28 And he left all, rose up, and followed him. 29 And Levi made him a great feast in his own house: and there was a great company of publicans and of others that sat down with them. 30 But their scribes and Pharisees murmured against his disciples, saying, Why do ye eat and drink with publicans and sinners? 31 And Jesus answering said unto them, They that are whole need not a physician; but they that are sick. 32 I came not to call the righteous, but sinners to repentance.

The religious people were offended when Jesus called sinners and even sat and ate with them. What the Pharisees and scribes were not aware of is that Jesus knew how to get sinners to follow him, and when they follow him, their lives will be saved.

Jesus expects more religious leaders to have a love for people, including sinners. Every effort must be made to allow sinners to come and know Jesus as their Lord.

No one is exempted from the call of the Lord. When Jesus calls people, he does not and will not discriminate against anyone. Believers must not make sinners feel that they are not worthy to come to know Jesus Christ.

So, the question is, has God called you? He has called everyone! God needs even those who have sinned to come unto him and have his blessing and protection.

2. Deny yourself and follow God

If you are going to go hard after God, then you must be willing to deny yourself some things and follow Christ. Some persons want the blessings of God, but they still want to follow the things which God wants them to deny themselves.

One reason why some persons are not blessed is that they are not going hard after God. When God called them, they kept thinking that they could still live their old lives.

However, the call of God requires everyone to make some changes to their lives. While they may not like many of the changes he requires of them, these changes are essential for their future success in God.

2.1 Take up your cross

Anyone who will deny themselves must be willing to take up their cross and follow the Lord. While this sounds like hard work, it is work that will bring great success for them.

Taking up the cross of Jesus is not an additional burden to anyone. It allows persons to walk away from sin and walk with the Lord.

Matthew 16:24-28

24 Then said Jesus unto his disciples, If any man will come after me, let him deny himself, and take up his cross, and follow me. 25 For whosoever will save his life shall lose it: and whosoever will lose his life for my sake shall find it. 26 For what is a man profited, if he shall gain the whole world, and lose his own soul? or what shall a man give in exchange for his soul? 27 For the Son of man shall come in the glory of his Father with his angels; and then he shall reward every man according to his works. 28 Verily I say unto you, There be some standing here, which shall not taste of death, till they see the Son of man coming in his kingdom.

Jesus asks some tough questions in this scripture. He wants every person to understand that whatever they do, they cannot save themselves. It makes no profit for persons to try in their own strength to save themselves, since their best effort will still see them losing their lives. Life is precious, and persons must follow the Lord.

2.2 Set yourself apart

When persons come to know the Lord as their Savior, they must be willing to set themselves apart. When they set themselves apart, they are allowing themselves to grow in the Lord.

Figure 1. Set yourself apart and gain more with the Lord

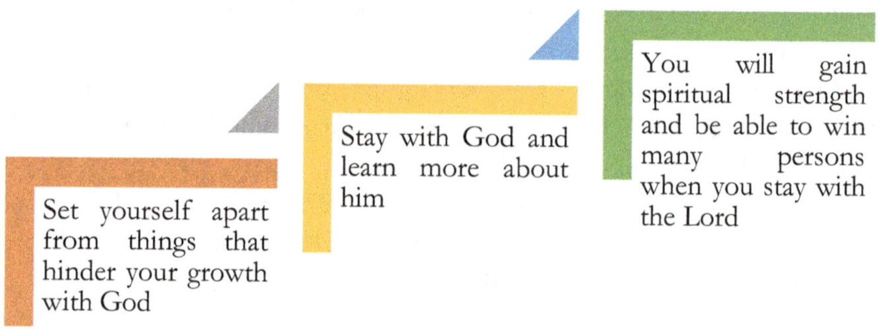

(All figures developed by the author unless otherwise noted.)

2.3 Commit your ways unto God

As persons deny themselves of some things, they must commit their ways unto the Lord. Proverbs 16:1-9 provides much guidance for believers. In verse 3, believers are reminded to commit their ways unto the Lord so that the Lord will establish them. This is a great assurance that when persons allow the Lord to work through them, they will be blessed.

Proverbs 16:1-9

1 The preparations of the heart in man, and the answer of the tongue, is from the LORD. 2 All the ways of a man are clean in his own eyes; but the LORD weigheth the spirits. 3 Commit thy works unto the LORD, and thy thoughts shall be established. 4 The LORD hath made all things for himself: yea, even the wicked for the day of evil. 5 Every one that is proud in heart is an abomination to the LORD: though hand join in hand, he shall not be unpunished. 6 By mercy and truth iniquity is purged: and by the fear of the LORD men depart from evil. ⁷When a man's ways please the LORD, he maketh even his enemies to be at peace with him. ⁸Better is a little with righteousness than great revenues without right. ⁹A man's heart deviseth his way: but the LORD directeth his steps.

It is God who prepares a man's heart, according to Proverbs 16:1. Therefore, everyone must allow the Lord to have full access to their heart. When a person gives their life to Christ, they are expected to allow him to flow through them, as he will. Those who try to hold back from the Lord will only be hurting their future.

Proverbs 16:2 provides a minor reflection, reminding persons that when they look at their own lives, they see everything being all right for them, but it is the Lord who weighs the spirit. Therefore, the answer from the Lord about a person's heart is greater than what a person thinks of himself or herself.

The Lord resists those who are proud in their hearts, according to Proverbs 16:5. Therefore, all those who come to know the Lord must deny themselves and follow the ways of the Lord.

Everyone has enemies. However, God is willing to contend with the enemies of the believers; therefore, the believers must commit themselves unto the Lord.

Many persons want to have peace with their enemies, and Proverbs 16:7 states that they can expect this peace if they commit their ways unto the Lord. No one knows the intention of the enemies but the Lord, so only he can defuse the enemies' plans against the lives of the believers.

Some people want to stay away from God because they are trying to secure their future independence. However, every person can devise their own strategy, but they must allow the Lord to direct their steps. If more persons allow the Lord to direct their steps, they will have great rewards and less stress.

3. Be intentional in seeking God first

As believers go hard after God, they must be intentional in following him. It must not be a choice, but a lifestyle where they follow God because they know of his goodness.

Psalm 145:18-20

18 The LORD is nigh unto all them that call upon him, to all that call upon him in truth. 19 He will fulfil the desire of them that fear him: he also will hear their cry, and will save them. 20 The LORD preserveth all them that love him: but all the wicked will he destroy.

How can people say that they cannot find God? He is always there and always willing to help those who seek him.

Psalm 107:13-14

13 Then they cried unto the LORD in their trouble, and he saved them out of their distresses. 14 He brought them out of darkness and the shadow of death, and brake their bands in sunder.

3.1 Why seek God first?

Everyone has the choice to decide what they will do. However, many believers have an understanding that they must seek God first. As they seek God first, he does many great things for them, as he has promised.

Matthew 6:33

33 But seek ye first the kingdom of God, and his righteousness; and all these things shall be added unto you.

Figure 2. Why believers must seek God first

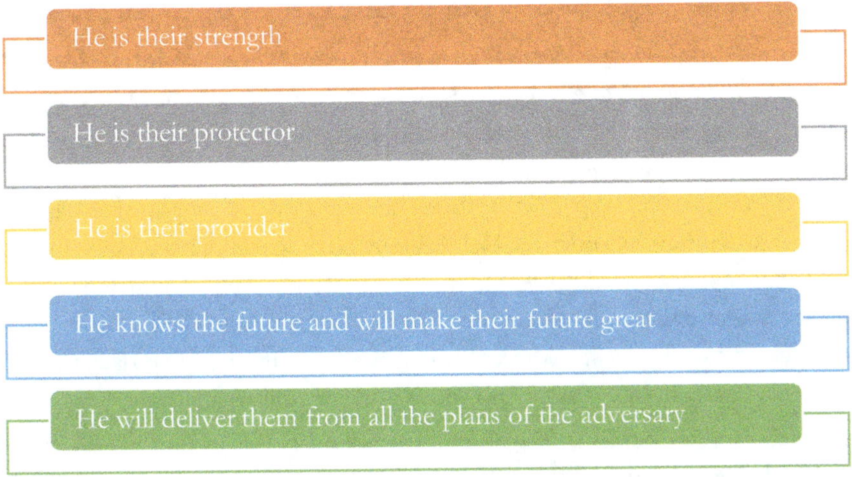

Anyone who wants to go hard after God must be willing to place him first in their life, and everything else will be subdued by him. Believers are never in a competition, but when God is on their side, they can be assured to have victories in areas that they had never thought about. God is constantly looking to do good things for his children as they envelop themselves in him.

3.2 Seek God early every day

God must be sought after daily. He is not a part-time God, but a God who is accessible daily to every person. In the scripture below, the psalmist indicates that he wants to see God's power and glory. Some persons are running away from God, and they are running into the hands of the adversary. However, when they seek God early, they can be assured that he will be there to protect them, as he demonstrates his power in and through their lives.

Psalm 63:1-11

1 O God, thou art my God; early will I seek thee: my soul thirsteth for thee, my flesh longeth for thee in a dry and thirsty land, where no water is; 2 To see thy power and thy glory, so as I have seen thee in the sanctuary. 3 Because thy lovingkindness is better than life, my lips shall praise thee. 4 Thus will I bless thee while I live: I will lift up my hands in thy name. 5 My soul shall be satisfied as with marrow and fatness; and my mouth shall praise thee with joyful lips: 6 When I remember thee upon my bed, and meditate on thee in the night watches.

7 Because thou hast been my help, therefore in the shadow of thy wings will I rejoice.

8 My soul followeth hard after thee: thy right hand upholdeth me. 9 But those that seek my soul, to destroy it, shall go into the lower parts of the earth. 10 They shall fall by the sword: they shall be a portion for foxes. 11 But the king shall rejoice in God; every one that sweareth by him shall glory: but the mouth of them that speak lies shall be stopped.

Psalm 63:4 reminds persons to bless the Lord while they are alive. This is further supported by verse 3, which says "my lips will praise thee."

When persons awake every day, they must place God first, ahead of everything else that they have to do. They must command their mornings to be blessed as they set Jesus to be in control of their day. Each day is filled with many challenges, but when God is first, he will navigate the believers' path. God will often provide avenues of escape for believers, allowing them to move from one day to the next.

God said in Proverbs 8:17 that those who seek him early will find him. Therefore, he is looking for persons to seek him.

Proverbs 8:17-19

17 I love them that love me; and those that seek me early shall find me. 18 Riches and honour are with me; yea, durable riches and righteousness. 19 My fruit is better than gold, yea, than fine gold; and my revenue than choice silver.

4. Cling to God

People have friends. Even Satan has friends.

However, those persons who are called by the Lord must cling unto him. It takes much effort to do this, but when an individual clings to the Lord, he will be there for them.

Every parent knows that their children will cling unto them when they are small. As soon as some parents move away from their children, those children will cry for them. Most children do not want their parents to leave them or anyone to take their parents away from them.

4.1 Zealously follow God

Psalm 63:8

8 My soul followeth hard after thee: thy right hand upholdeth me.

The writer of this verse states that his soul follows hard after God. It is therefore evident that he is zealous to follow the Lord. Those who want more of God must be willing to keep going after him, as those who have a lackadaisical approach cannot expect anything great from God.

Believers must have a private relationship with God, and in this private relationship, they must go hard after God. Even when no one is looking, they must constantly seek God.

Every believer will go through challenges. There are times when the unsaved may question the believer's faith and may ask them, as in Psalm 42:3, "Where is your God?" However, the believer must not be despondent, but continue to follow God.

Psalm 42:1-3

1 As the hart panteth after the water brooks, so panteth my soul after thee, O God. 2 My soul thirsteth for God, for the living God: when shall I come and appear before God? 3 My tears have been my meat day and night, while they continually say unto me, Where is thy God?

Anyone who has gone without water for some period will know how water is to their thirst. The writer of Psalm 42:2 says, "My soul thirsts for God," showing deep affection for God. If many persons were so zealous for God, then they would have seen the hands of God operating greatly in their lives.

How many believers have spent time seeking God in which they cry in his presence? This deep affection for God is more than just coming into his presence and hoping that he may do something for the believer whenever he feels like it. Psalm 42:3 shows the writer constantly weeping in the presence of the Lord, such that his tears have become meat for both night and day.

4.2 Firmly connect to the source

As Jesus walked the earth, he showed his relationship with the Father. He never sought to distance himself from the Lord. Many of the things he spoke about showed his connection with the Father.

Jesus wants every believer to be connected with the source. He knows that many persons need God in their lives, but they are trying to use other alternatives. Anyone who wants God the Father has no other alternatives but to go through Christ.

John 15:1-8

1 I am the true vine, and my Father is the husbandman. 2 Every branch in me that beareth not fruit he taketh away: and every branch that beareth fruit, he purgeth it, that it may bring forth more fruit. 3 Now ye are clean through the word which I have spoken unto you. 4 Abide in me, and I in you. As the branch cannot bear fruit of itself, except it abide in the vine; no more can ye, except ye abide in me. 5 I am the vine, ye are the branches: He that abideth in me, and I in him, the same bringeth forth much fruit: for without me ye can do nothing. 6 If a man abide not in me, he is cast forth as a branch, and is withered; and men gather them, and cast them into the fire, and they are burned. 7 If ye abide in me, and my words abide in you, ye shall ask what ye will, and it shall be done unto you. 8 Herein is my Father glorified, that ye bear much fruit; so shall ye be my disciples.

Figure 3. Believers who want their lives to be effective must come through Jesus

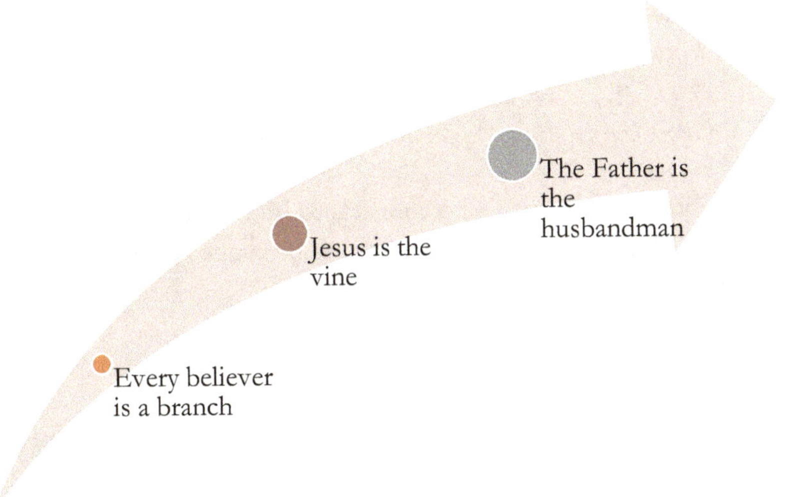

No believer can skip this process and get to the Father without Jesus' involvement. When Jesus came to earth, he came to reconcile sinners unto the Father. Therefore, Jesus is not competing with the Father, but he is there to help believers to find their way to God through him. The Father is referred to as the husbandman, as per John 15:1. In his role as the husbandman, the Father will cleanse all believers and make their lives effective.

4.3 Jesus is the way to the Father

As Jesus taught his disciples, they wanted to see the Father. Jesus gave them a surprising response, according to John 14:9. They were not expecting this answer, but it was the only answer Jesus had to their concern.

John 14:5-14

5 Thomas saith unto him, Lord, we know not whither thou goest; and how can we know the way? 6 Jesus saith unto him, I am the way, the truth, and the life: no man cometh unto the Father, but by me. 7 If ye had known me, ye should have known my Father also: and from henceforth ye know him, and have seen him. 8 Philip saith unto him, Lord, show us the Father, and it sufficeth us. 9 Jesus saith unto him, Have I been so long time with you, and yet hast thou not known me, Philip? he that hath seen me hath seen the Father; and how sayest thou then, Show us the Father? 10 Believest thou not that I am in the Father, and the Father in me? the words that I speak unto you I speak not of myself: but the Father that dwelleth in me, he doeth the works. 11 Believe me that I am in the Father, and the Father in me: or else believe me for the very works' sake. 12 Verily, verily, I say unto you, He that believeth on me, the works that I do shall he do also; and greater works than these shall he do; because I go unto my Father. 13 And whatsoever ye shall ask in my name, that will I do, that the Father may be glorified in the Son. 14 If ye shall ask any thing in my name, I will do it.

Therefore, every believer who connects to Jesus connects to the Father. Jesus is available to all believers who want to be connected to the Father, at any time of the day.

5. Equip yourself with prayers

No one can build a relationship with God without prayer. Jesus constantly prayed throughout his earthly ministry. Since Jesus is the Son of God and had direct access to him, yet considered it important to pray regularly, how can believers expect to live a life without prayer?

5.1 Jesus started his earthly ministry with prayer

When Jesus was ready to start his earthly ministry after his baptism, he went into the wilderness and prayed. Many persons may not take the same approach as Jesus. Some persons will prefer to start their ministry first, and if they fail, then they will pray. However, Jesus prayed first, and immediately he had success through his ministry, despite the many challenges he faced and the obstacles he needed to overcome.

Matthew 4:1-11

1 Then was Jesus led up of the Spirit into the wilderness to be tempted of the devil. 2 And when he had fasted forty days and forty nights, he was afterward an hungred. 3 And when the tempter came to him, he said, If thou be the Son of God, command that these stones be made bread. 4 But he answered and said, It is written, Man shall not live by bread alone, but by every word that proceedeth out of the mouth of God. 5 Then the devil taketh him up into the holy city, and setteth him on a pinnacle of the temple, 6 And saith unto him, If thou be the Son of God, cast thyself down: for it is written, He shall give his angels charge concerning thee: and in their hands they shall bear thee up, lest at any time thou dash thy foot against a stone. 7 Jesus said unto him, It is written again, Thou shalt not tempt the Lord thy God. 8 Again, the devil taketh him up into an exceeding high mountain, and sheweth him all the kingdoms of the world, and the glory of them; 9 And saith unto him, All these things will I give thee, if thou wilt fall down and worship me. 10 Then saith Jesus unto him, Get thee hence, Satan: for it is written, Thou shalt worship the Lord thy God, and him only shalt thou serve. ¹¹ Then the devil leaveth him, and, behold, angels came and ministered unto him.

Take note that after Jesus was baptized, he was led up into the wilderness. A question to many believers is "Who is leading you?" If it is the Holy Spirit, then you are on the right path to victory. Wherever God is willing to lead you as a believer, be willing to follow, since he will only lead you in the right direction.

Jesus fasted and prayed. Along with the Holy Spirit, through fasting and prayer, Jesus was willing to take on the devil, as he knew that he was equipped. Throughout Matthew 4:1-11, Satan tempted Jesus three times, and Satan was unsuccessful in all of his attempts. Jesus always had the antidote to Satan's question.

Believers have much ammunition at their disposal when they pray. The adversary will not conquer a believer who has sought God and has God on their side. In Psalm 34:4, the psalmist sought the Lord, and the Lord heard and answered the psalmist's prayer. Therefore, when believers seek God, they must expect that he will hear and answer their prayers.

Psalm 34:1-4

¹ I will bless the LORD at all times: his praise shall continually be in my mouth. ² My soul shall make her boast in the LORD: the humble shall hear thereof, and be glad. ³ O magnify the LORD with me, and let us exalt his name together. ⁴ I sought the LORD, and he heard me, and delivered me from all my fears.

Satan thought that Jesus was vulnerable because he was alone and had been without food for forty days. However, Jesus was better equipped to combat the adversary because he spent more time seeking God and more time in prayer.

5.2 Jesus taught his disciples to pray

The disciples saw the success of Jesus, and they asked him to teach them to pray. Jesus was willing to teach them to pray, since he knew that once their lives were guarded with prayer, then they will have success.

Matthew 6:9-15

⁹ After this manner therefore pray ye: Our Father which art in heaven, Hallowed be thy name. ¹⁰ Thy kingdom come, Thy will be done in earth, as it is in heaven. ¹¹ Give us this day our daily bread. ¹² And forgive us our debts, as we forgive our debtors. ¹³ And lead us not into temptation, but deliver us from evil: For thine is the kingdom, and the power, and the glory, forever. Amen. ¹⁴ For if ye forgive men their trespasses, your heavenly Father will also forgive you: 15 But if ye forgive not men their trespasses, neither will your Father forgive your trespasses.

Jesus took time to teach his disciples to pray. The prayer he taught them was simple but profound. While the prayer to the disciples many centuries ago, it is still applicable to modern-day society.

Jesus taught believers not to have a selfish prayer, but a global prayer. Therefore, when believers are praying, they must consider the entire world and not pray in hatred.

5.3 Combat principalities and powers through prayer

The life of every believer will be faced with challenges and obstacles from the adversary. If believers do not encounter regular challenges from the adversary, then they are in bed with the adversary. Satan plans to derail all believers and will never allow them to succeed without placing obstacles in their paths. Nevertheless, every believer must win against Satan through prayer.

When Apostle Paul wrote Ephesians while he was in prison, he wanted every believer to be properly protected from the adversary. Satan knows that some believers will go hard after God, so he wants to stop them, and to stop them very early.

However, as Satan plans, believers must not give him opportunities to execute his plans. The believers cannot win against Satan in their own strength, but only through Christ. While you might have read Ephesians 6:10-18 before, you must reexamine this scripture and properly prepare yourself for Satan.

Ephesians 6:10-18

10 Finally, my brethren, be strong in the Lord, and in the power of his might. 11 Put on the whole armour of God, that ye may be able to stand against the wiles of the devil. 12 For we wrestle not against flesh and blood, but against principalities, against powers, against the rulers of the darkness of this world, against spiritual wickedness in high places. 13 Wherefore take unto you the whole armour of God, that ye may be able to withstand in the evil day, and having done all, to stand. 14 Stand therefore, having your loins girt about with truth, and having on the breastplate of righteousness; 15 And your feet shod with the preparation of the gospel of peace; 16 Above all, taking the shield of faith, wherewith ye shall be able to quench all the fiery darts of the wicked. 17 And take the helmet of salvation, and the sword of the Spirit, which is the word of God:

18 Praying always with all prayer and supplication in the Spirit, and watching thereunto with all perseverance and supplication for all saints.

Apostle Paul did not ask the believers to put on part of their armor, but their whole armor, according to Ephesians 6:11. He knew that the adversary would attack them from all angles. Therefore, those believers who are less prepared will be easily distracted and lose their battle against the adversary.

The adversary against which believers wrestle is not a physical person. Therefore, the physical strength of the believer is no match against a spiritual adversary, according to Ephesians 6:12. This spiritual wickedness is in high places. So, although believers may want to look down, expecting that the adversary is powerless and only operates from the ground, they need to look up, as the adversary will operate from high levels to destroy them.

Satan will throw darts at every believer, and those who do not have on the full armor will be hurt by those darts. The Apostle Paul wanted to tell believers to gird up their loins with the truth.

5.4 Pray regularly

Jesus states that believers must not only have faith, but pray as well. Many times, when persons see certain challenges, they may lose faith. However, Jesus states that they must pray and not faint.

Luke 18:1

1 And he spake a parable unto them to this end, that men ought always to pray, and not to faint.

If believers have no faith, then they will place themselves in a state of defeat. Jesus is calling for more believers to pray, and for them to pray today and not wait until tomorrow.

5.5 Fasting and prayer empower believers

A man was very concerned about the deliverance of his son. He brought his demon-possessed son to the disciples, but the disciples could not help him. The man eventually got Jesus' attention, since the man did not want to take his son home while he was still demon-possessed.

Jesus, always being merciful, rebuked the demon from the young man. The boy's father was relieved that his son was delivered. The disciples came to Jesus privately and asked him how he was able to do something that they were unable to do. Jesus, being a good teacher, told the disciples that this kind does not go out but through prayer and fasting.

Matthew 17:14-21

14 And when they were come to the multitude, there came to him a certain man, kneeling down to him, and saying, 15 Lord, have mercy on my son: for he is lunatick, and sore vexed: for ofttimes he falleth into the fire, and oft into the water. 16 And I brought him to thy disciples, and they could not cure him. 17 Then Jesus answered and said, O faithless and perverse generation, how long shall I be with you? how long shall I suffer you? bring him hither to me. 18 And Jesus rebuked the devil; and he departed out of him: and the child was cured from that very hour. 19 Then came the disciples to Jesus apart, and said, Why could not we cast him out? 20 And Jesus said unto them, Because of your unbelief: for verily I say unto you, If ye have faith as a grain of mustard seed, ye shall say unto this mountain, Remove hence to yonder place; and it shall remove; and nothing shall be impossible unto you. 21 Howbeit this kind goeth not out but by prayer and fasting.

All believers must make prayer a quintessential element of their lives. Many persons are demon-possessed, but with prayer and fasting, God will bring deliverance to their lives.

6. Fervent prayer unto God

Every believer is called to live a life of prayer. However, their prayer must have fervency.

God wants to see every believer going hard after him in prayer. When they approach him in prayer, they are expecting him to show up on their behalf. They are not willing to leave his presence until they receive an answer to their prayer.

As James admonished the believers, he spoke to them about prayer. There will often be persons who are afflicted, and prayers must be said for them. Besides prayer, he encouraged persons to sing psalms. When persons worship God through prayer and praise, they must expect that God will make his presence and power known among them.

James 5:13-18

13 Is any among you afflicted? let him pray. Is any merry? let him sing psalms. 14 Is any sick among you? let him call for the elders of the church; and let them pray over him, anointing him with oil in the name of the Lord: 15 And the prayer of faith shall save the sick, and the Lord shall raise him up; and if he have committed sins, they shall be forgiven him. 16 Confess your faults one to another, and pray one for another, that ye may be healed. The effectual fervent prayer of a righteous man availeth much. 17 Elias was a man subject to like passions as we are, and he prayed earnestly that it might not rain: and it rained not on the earth by the space of three years and six months. 18 And he prayed again, and the heaven gave rain, and the earth brought forth her fruit.

Elijah was a human just like everyone else. However, he knew the power of God. He was willing to prove the God whom he served, as he showed great confidence in his God.

Rain often happens as a natural event, after evaporation and condensation take place. When the cloud is filled, it is expected to rain. However, Elijah did not wait for all of those events to happen; instead, he was willing to go hard after God for the Lord to release rain. He was fervent in his prayer, and

God answered his prayer. If Elijah was willing to command that it rain, and God answered his prayer, then why should believers not expect God to do similar things and work miracles for them?

For further details of the story of Elijah and his prayer, please see 1 Kings 18:41-46. Notice that Elijah had challenged King Ahab that the Lord would answer his prayer.

1 Kings 18:41-46

41 And Elijah said unto Ahab, Get thee up, eat and drink; for there is a sound of abundance of rain. 42 So Ahab went up to eat and to drink. And Elijah went up to the top of Carmel; and he cast himself down upon the earth, and put his face between his knees, 43 And said to his servant, Go up now, look toward the sea. And he went up, and looked, and said, There is nothing. And he said, Go again seven times. 44 And it came to pass at the seventh time, that he said, Behold, there ariseth a little cloud out of the sea, like a man's hand. And he said, Go up, say unto Ahab, Prepare thy chariot, and get thee down that the rain stop thee not. 45 And it came to pass in the mean while, that the heaven was black with clouds and wind, and there was a great rain. And Ahab rode, and went to Jezreel. 46 And the hand of the LORD was on Elijah, and he girded up his loins, and ran before Ahab to the entrance of Jezreel.

When believers exercise their faith like Elijah, then many great things will happen for them. God is often waiting for his children to approach him in confidence.

Mark 9:23

23 Jesus said unto him, If thou canst believe, all things are possible to him that believeth.

Jesus reminded believers that all things are possible if they only believe. Those who believe God must be willing to put their faith in action and pray that God will do great things for them. Prayer has the ability to make the impossible, possible.

7. Equip yourself with the word

Every believer who is zealous for God and the things of God must know God's word. It is through the word of God and through their own testimonies that believers will be able to overcome the enemy.

Within some congregations, members may believe that they have to give more attention to their leaders and less attention to the word of God. However, that format will only lead to disaster. One element of the growth of believers is for them to place God at the pinnacle of their lives and to follow his word diligently.

7.1 Believers are equipped to overcome the enemy

Every believer will go through tough times. However, those who remain in God will have victories. Their victory is not because of their strength and wisdom, but because they have placed God first in their lives and believed his word. No believer can combat the adversary and win in their own strength. Therefore, every day, believers must cloak themselves in the presence of God.

Revelation 12:10-12

10 And I heard a loud voice saying in heaven, Now is come salvation, and strength, and the kingdom of our God, and the power of his Christ: for the accuser of our brethren is cast down, which accused them before our God day and night. 11 And they overcame him by the blood of the Lamb, and by the word of their testimony; and they loved not their lives unto the death. 12 Therefore rejoice, ye heavens, and ye that dwell in them. Woe to the inhabiters of the earth and of the sea! for the devil is come down unto you, having great wrath, because he knoweth that he hath but a short time.

7.2 Faith comes through God's word

Many believers are constantly asking God for more faith. However, every believer has work to do if they want their faith to be strengthened. They must go after the word of God so that their faith will grow.

When persons have just accepted the Lord, their faith is often weak. For persons who have lost a loved one or who suddenly lose their jobs, their faith sometimes becomes weak. To help strengthen their faith, they must go to the word of God, not whenever they feel like it, but as their daily diet.

Romans 10:14-17

14 How then shall they call on him in whom they have not believed? and how shall they believe in him of whom they have not heard? and how shall they hear without a preacher? 15 And how shall they preach, except they be sent? as it is written, How beautiful are the feet of them that preach the gospel of peace, and bring glad tidings of good things! 16 But they have not all obeyed the gospel. For Esaias saith, Lord, who hath believed our report? 17 So then faith cometh by hearing, and hearing by the word of God.

7.3 An approved worker for God

The Apostle Paul teaches believers that for them to be approved workers of the Lord, they need to know his word. This teaching is also evident in many professional institutions. When employees start to work for an organization, they are sometimes provided with an orientation session or given an employee manual to read. As the employees become more aware of the organization and its culture, then they are equipped to start actual work for the organization. The orientation session can be for some hours, or it may be for several days. Technical jobs often require longer training periods.

Many manufacturers provide manuals for use of the equipment. Once the user of the equipment reads the manual and understands what has to be done, then they can proceed to the next stage and start to use the equipment.

God wants every believer to embrace a similar approach and strategy. He wants his children to know his word so that they can rightly present his word in every situation.

2 Timothy 2:13-15

13 If we believe not, yet he abideth faithful: he cannot deny himself. 14 Of these things put them in remembrance, charging them before the Lord that they strive not about words to no profit, but to the subverting of the hearers. 15 Study to shew thyself approved unto God, a workman that needeth not to be ashamed, rightly dividing the word of truth.

Believers must be aware that they must be so equipped that they can rightly divide the word of truth. It takes a great understanding of God's word to place information in context and content.

Figure 4. Benefits of studying God's word

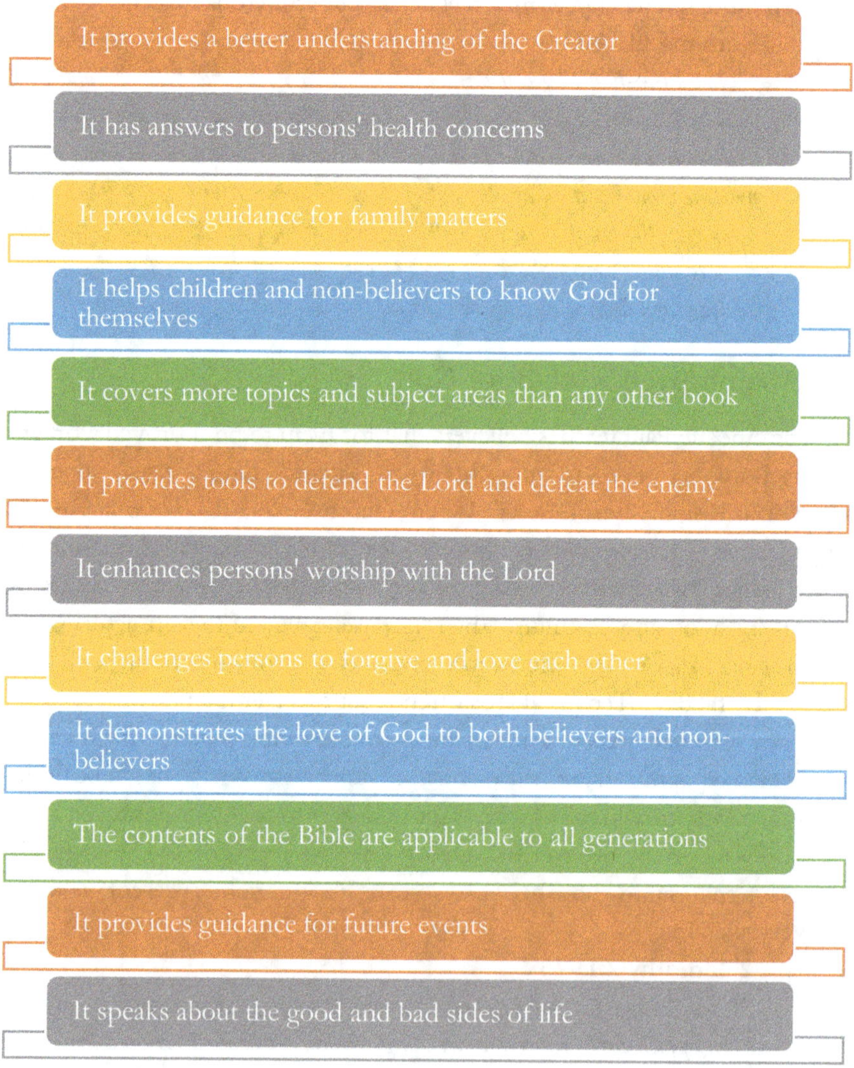

It provides a better understanding of the Creator

It has answers to persons' health concerns

It provides guidance for family matters

It helps children and non-believers to know God for themselves

It covers more topics and subject areas than any other book

It provides tools to defend the Lord and defeat the enemy

It enhances persons' worship with the Lord

It challenges persons to forgive and love each other

It demonstrates the love of God to both believers and non-believers

The contents of the Bible are applicable to all generations

It provides guidance for future events

It speaks about the good and bad sides of life

It is often seen that persons have misapplied certain scriptures and believe that they are doing a good thing for God. However, while they may sound good to themselves, they will be unable to impact the adversary when they misapply God's word.

7.4 Meditate on his word

Many persons who have attended some formal learning will know that there is a difference between reading information and assimilating it. God intends that every believer will spend much time mediating and applying his word correctly.

As believers mediate on God's word, they sharpen their skills and become familiar with God's promises. They know what God wants them to have and what they must stay away from.

Psalm 1:1-3

1 Blessed is the man that walketh not in the counsel of the ungodly, nor standeth in the way of sinners, nor sitteth in the seat of the scornful. 2 But his delight is in the law of the LORD; and in his law doth he meditate day and night. 3 And he shall be like a tree planted by the rivers of water, that bringeth forth his fruit in his season; his leaf also shall not wither; and whatsoever he doeth shall prosper.

Verse 2 talks about the believer's delight being in the laws of God. The believer is expected to mediate on God's laws, and God will make them like a tree planted by the rivers of water. When more believers mediate on God's law, the world will see the blessings of God on their lives, as the believers will prosper in difficult economic situations since God is their source.

Figure 5. Benefits for believers who meditate on God's word; Psalm 1:3

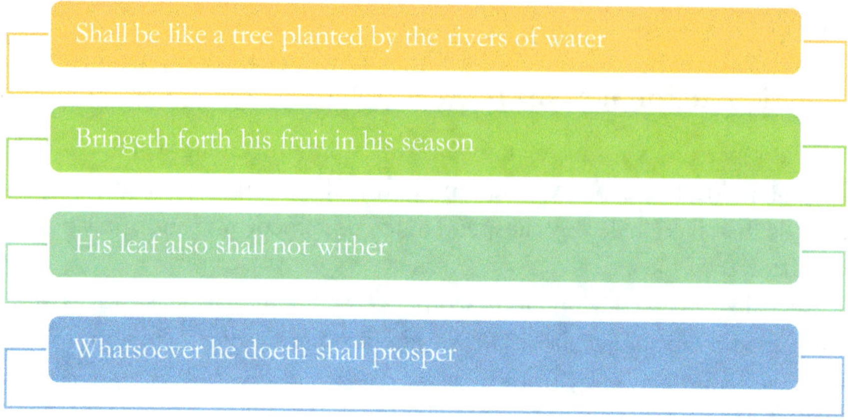

Believers must make more time to know God's law. Their lives will become better as they know God's laws and apply them to their everyday lives. God intends to bless every believer, but the believers must be willing to equip themselves with his word.

Joshua, a servant of God, was reminded that he must be strong and courageous. In so doing, he had to gird up himself with God's word. God told Joshua not to turn from the law which was given to Moses. This was a strong statement to Joshua as he took over from Moses, his leader.

Joshua 1:7-8

7 Only be thou strong and very courageous, that thou mayest observe to do according to all the law, which Moses my servant commanded thee: turn not from it to the right hand or to the left, that thou mayest prosper withersoever thou goest. 8 This book of the law shall not depart out of thy mouth; but thou shalt meditate therein day and night, that thou mayest observe to do according to all that is written therein: for then thou shalt make thy way prosperous, and then thou shalt have good success.

As God worked through Moses, there were many successes. Those successes were possible because Moses listened to God, trusted his words, and applied those words to whatever situation confronted him. Joshua could expect similar successes if he meditated on God's laws and did things similar to Moses.

7.5 His word is a light

Every believer will have to pass through dark patches in their lives. As they go through those dark patches, they will need some light. Each believer has the responsibility of recharging their batteries as they spend time knowing more about God's word. His words are sweet, and they enlighten believers.

Psalm 119:103-105

103 How sweet are thy words unto my taste! yea, sweeter than honey to my mouth!

104 Through thy precepts I get understanding: therefore I hate every false way.

105 Thy word is a lamp unto my feet, and a light unto my path.

God's word provides light to believers' feet and a light unto their path. Therefore, they should not stumble when they act according to God's word. The word of God is not for only some situations; it is applicable to all situations.

More believers need to equip themselves with God's word. While they may not always feel like doing so, they must see it as their responsibility if they want to go hard after God.

7.6 What must believers do with God's word?

There are many things that people can do with God's word. However, believers have some particularly important things that they can do with God's word.

Figure 6. What to do with the word of the Lord?

Study it	Hide it in your heart	Meditate on it	Apply it
• 2 Timothy 2:15	• Psalm 119:11	• Joshua 1:7-8	• 2 Timothy 2:15, Joshua 1:7-8

Besides reading and mediating on God's word, believers must apply the word. Too often, believers attend church services and receive God's word, but fail to apply what they learn.

7.7 Hide his word in your heart

Believers must remember that God's word is not a trophy. It is an important tool to be used by every believer in their everyday life and in every situation. Therefore, those who have made God's word into a trophy must begin to apply this important resource every day, just as they need food to survive.

Figure 7. The resting place of God's word for the believer

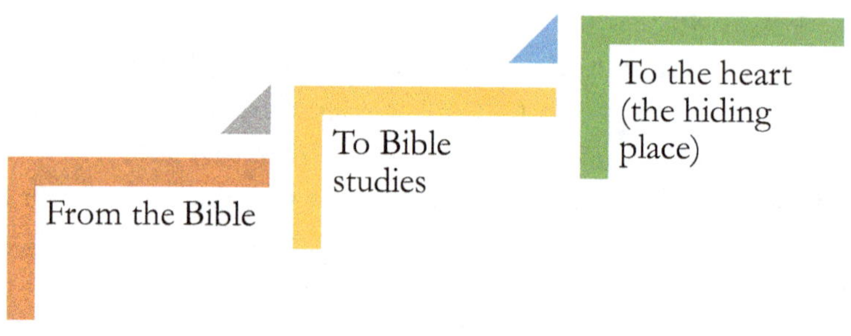

If a believer wants to become stronger, they must be willing to attend church services and learn more of God's word. They can also listen to teachings of God's word, which may be available through online options and electronic devices. They must place God's word in their heart so that whenever a situation confronts them, they do not have to go in search of the word, but can search within their heart and apply God's word.

Psalm 119:11

11 Thy word have I hid in mine heart, that I might not sin against thee.

Figure 8. Why hide God's word in your heart?

It is easy to access

Every believer needs their heart connected to the Lord (as they need the word of the Lord to do his work)

Wherever persons go, their heart goes with them (so the word goes with them wherever they go)

The heart supplies blood to every part of the body (and will send the word to all parts of a believer's life)

The heart is always active, even when persons are asleep (the word remains with the believer even in the quiet moments)

The heart changes its beat based upon the demand (so the word will be applied based upon the situation)

Every believer must be so equipped with God's word that they need little assistance in applying the word correctly. They must be ready for any sudden attack by the adversary, and they must always surprise the adversary with their understanding and application of God's word.

8. God's work requires his Spirit

The works that believers have to do cannot be effectively completed in their own strength. Many persons are trying daily in their own strength, but they are failing. One of the reasons why they are failing is that they do not have the Holy Spirit with them to make their work easy.

Zechariah 4:6

6 Then he answered and spake unto me, saying, This is the word of the LORD unto Zerubbabel, saying, Not by might, nor by power, but by my spirit, saith the LORD of hosts.

In this discussion between Zechariah and the angel, the angel told him that is "not by might, nor by power, but by the spirit." Every believer must be reminded that the work they are called to do requires more than human strength and wisdom.

8.1 Believers are promised the Comforter

The earthly ministry of Jesus was coming to an end. He knew that when he departed from the earth, the work of his Father must continue. The disciples would need additional strength and wisdom to do God's work. Therefore, he announced to the believers that they will be provided with great support in order to continue his Father's work.

John 14:15-27

15 If ye love me, keep my commandments. 16 And I will pray the Father, and he shall give you another Comforter, that he may abide with you for ever; 17 Even the Spirit of truth; whom the world cannot receive, because it seeth him not, neither knoweth him: but ye know him; for he dwelleth with you, and shall be in you. 18 I will not leave you comfortless: I will come to you. 19 Yet a little while, and the world seeth me no more; but ye see me: because I live, ye shall live also. 20 At that day ye shall know that I am in my Father, and ye in me, and I in you. 21 He that hath my commandments, and keepeth them, he it is that loveth me: and he that loveth me shall be loved of my Father, and I will love him, and will manifest myself to him.

22 Judas saith unto him, not Iscariot, Lord, how is it that thou wilt manifest thyself unto us, and not unto the world? 23 Jesus answered and said unto him, If a man love me, he will keep my words: and my Father will love him, and we will come unto him, and make our abode with him. 24 He that loveth me not keepeth not my sayings: and the word which ye hear is not mine, but the Father's which sent me. 25 These things have I spoken unto you, being yet present with you. 26 But the Comforter, which is the Holy Ghost, whom the Father will send in my name, he shall teach you all things, and bring all things to your remembrance, whatsoever I have said unto you. 27 Peace I leave with you, my peace I give unto you: not as the world giveth, give I unto you. Let not your heart be troubled, neither let it be afraid.

There are many things that the Holy Spirit wants to do for believers. However, each believer must go after God for him to empower them with his Spirit. The Holy Spirit will come upon persons who need him and those who are working for the Lord. When the Holy Spirit comes, he will teach people all things and will also bring to their remembrance whatever the Lord spoke to them (John 14:26). When persons are experiencing a bad day, they sometimes forget what has been promised to them. They forget that better days are ahead of them. So, when the Holy Spirit comes into the lives of believers, he will remind them of the many promises of God and will comfort their hearts.

Every believer should be yearning for the Holy Spirit. While believers must be excited about the works which they have to do for the Lord, they must also seek to equip themselves with the Holy Spirit.

8.2 Jesus' earthly ministry started with the Spirit

When Jesus was ready for his earthly ministry, he ensured that he had the Spirit with him. After Jesus received the Spirit, his work on earth was efficient and effective. In less than four years, Jesus's earthly ministry was completed and he experienced unprecedented success.

Matthew 3:13-17

13 Then cometh Jesus from Galilee to Jordan unto John, to be baptized of him. 14 But John forbad him, saying, I have need to be baptized of thee, and comest thou to me? 15 And Jesus answering said unto him, Suffer it to be so now: for thus it becometh us to fulfil all righteousness. Then he suffered him. 16 And Jesus, when he was baptized, went up straightway out of the water: and, lo, the heavens were opened unto him, and he saw the Spirit of God descending like a dove, and lighting upon him: 17 And lo a voice from heaven, saying, This is my beloved Son, in whom I am well pleased.

Immediately after Jesus was baptized, the Spirit came upon him, according to Matthew 3:16. After Jesus received the Spirit, he went into the wilderness in a time of prayer. Jesus understood that if anyone is going to go hard after God, they need his spirit for the ministry which is set before them.

8.3 Jesus departed, but the Holy Spirit will come

Before Jesus departed from his followers for the last time, he met with his disciples. As he was talking to them, they saw when he was ascended. Many of them might have become worried and lost hope. However, they continued in prayer and waited for the promise of the Holy Spirit which Jesus had given them.

Acts 1:1-14

1 The former treatise have I made, O Theophilus, of all that Jesus began both to do and teach, 2 Until the day in which he was taken up, after that he through the Holy Ghost had given commandments unto the apostles whom he had chosen: 3 To whom also he shewed himself alive after his passion by many infallible proofs, being seen of them forty days, and speaking of the things pertaining to the kingdom of God: 4 And, being assembled together with them, commanded them that they should not depart from Jerusalem, but wait for the promise of the Father, which, saith he, ye have heard of me. 5 For John truly baptized with water; but ye shall be baptized with the Holy Ghost not many days hence.

6 When they therefore were come together, they asked of him, saying, Lord, wilt thou at this time restore again the kingdom to Israel? 7 And he said unto them, It is not for you to know the times or the seasons, which the Father hath put in his own power. 8 But ye shall receive power, after that the Holy Ghost is come upon you: and ye shall be witnesses unto me both in Jerusalem, and in all Judaea, and in Samaria, and unto the uttermost part of the earth. 9 And when he had spoken these things, while they beheld, he was taken up; and a cloud received him out of their sight. 10 And while they looked stedfastly toward heaven as he went up, behold, two men stood by them in white apparel; 11 Which also said, Ye men of Galilee, why stand ye gazing up into heaven? this same Jesus, which is taken up from you into heaven, shall so come in like manner as ye have seen him go into heaven.

12 Then returned they unto Jerusalem from the mount called Olivet, which is from Jerusalem a sabbath day's journey. 13 And when they were come in, they went up into an upper room, where abode both Peter, and James, and John, and Andrew, Philip, and Thomas, Bartholomew, and Matthew, James the son of Alphaeus, and Simon Zelotes, and Judas the brother of James. 14 These all continued with one accord in prayer and supplication, with the women, and Mary the mother of Jesus, and with his brethren.

The disciples were willing to go hard after God, but they were waiting in the upper room for the infilling of the Holy Spirit. As they waited, they continued in prayer, strengthening each other in the faith.

God will always fulfill his promise. Indeed, the Holy Spirit came upon those who were waiting in the upper room, and their lives were changed forever. Thank God for his Holy Spirit.

9. Seek spiritual gifts

All believers ought to seek spiritual gifts, which are available through the Holy Spirit. There is no price associated with seeking the Holy Spirit. The Holy Spirit is free of cost and will always be available to all believers who need him.

Figure 9. Why believers must seek the Holy Spirit

He was promised to the believers

He is free of cost

He will teach believers all truth

He is a member of the Godhead

The believer's ministry will be effective with his help

The Holy Spirit will convict persons of their sins

Signs and wonderful blessings will flow through the believer's life

Things that happen in heaven will be revealed to the believers

Believers will have power over Satan and his workers

The information provided in the diagram above shows that all believers who do not have the Holy Spirit should become desperate and seek this Holy Spirit which Jesus promised them. Life will be better for all those who have received the Holy Spirit. While believers will still face persecution and the adversary, they will be assured that God will be there for them and give them victories.

9.1 Spiritual gifts available to all believers

The Apostle Paul reminds believers to covet the best gifts, according to 1 Corinthians 12:31. He wanted the believers to be zealous and seek those spiritual gifts which the Lord had promised. No one individual will have all the spiritual gifts. However, believers are expected to work together, before and after they receive the spiritual gifts. No spiritual gift is superior to any other.

1 Corinthians 12:1-31

1 Now concerning spiritual gifts, brethren, I would not have you ignorant. 2 Ye know that ye were Gentiles, carried away unto these dumb idols, even as ye were led. 3 Wherefore I give you to understand, that no man speaking by the Spirit of God calleth Jesus accursed: and that no man can say that Jesus is the Lord, but by the Holy Ghost. 4 Now there are diversities of gifts, but the same Spirit. 5 And there are differences of administrations, but the same Lord. 6 And there are diversities of operations, but it is the same God which worketh all in all. 7 But the manifestation of the Spirit is given to every man to profit withal.

8 For to one is given by the Spirit the word of wisdom; to another the word of knowledge by the same Spirit; 9 To another faith by the same Spirit; to another the gifts of healing by the same Spirit; 10 To another the working of miracles; to another prophecy; to another discerning of spirits; to another divers kind of tongues; to another the interpretation of tongues: 11 But all these worketh that one and the selfsame Spirit, dividing to every man severally as he will. 12 For as the body is one, and hath many members, and all the members of that one body, being many, are one body: so also is Christ. 13 For by one Spirit are we all baptized into one body, whether we be Jews or Gentiles, whether we be bond or free; and have been all made to drink into one Spirit. 14 For the body is not one member, but many.

15 If the foot shall say, Because I am not the hand, I am not of the body; is it therefore not of the body? 16 And if the ear shall say, Because I am not the eye, I am not of the body; is it therefore not of the body? 17 If the whole body were an eye, where were the hearing? If the whole were hearing, where were the smelling? 18 But now hath God set the members every one of them in the body, as it hath pleased him. 19 And if they were all one member, where were the body? 20 But now are they many members, yet but one body. 21 And the eye cannot say unto the hand, I have no need of thee: nor again the head to the feet, I have no need of you.

22 Nay, much more those members of the body, which seem to be more feeble, are necessary: 23 And those members of the body, which we think to be less honourable, upon these we bestow more abundant honour; and our uncomely parts have more abundant comeliness. 24 For our comely parts have no need: but God hath tempered the body together, having given more abundant honour to that part which lacked. 25 That there should be no schism in the body; but that the members should have the same care one for another. 26 And whether one member suffer, all the members suffer with it; or one member be honoured, all the members rejoice with it.

27 Now ye are the body of Christ, and members in particular. 28 And God hath set some in the church, first apostles, secondarily prophets, thirdly teachers, after that miracles, then gifts of healings, helps, governments, diversities of tongues. 29 Are all apostles? are all prophets? are all teachers? Are all workers of miracles? 30 Have all the gifts of healing? do all speak with tongues? do all interpret? 31 But covet earnestly the best gifts: and yet shew I unto you a more excellent way.

No believer should be empty-handed concerning spiritual gifts. Those persons who have just given their lives to the Lord can expect to have the Holy Spirit, just like those who have been serving the Lord for many years.

10. Spiritual gifts produce positive results

Persons may sometimes want to defend their reasons why they have not gone hard after God for his Holy Spirit so that they will receive spiritual gifts. Nevertheless, when believers have spiritual gifts, they must expect that signs and wonders will follow their lives.

These spiritual gifts are not passive gifts but gifts to be activated in the lives of believers.

When the Apostle Paul went to Ephesus, he met some of the disciples and asked them if they had received the Holy Spirit; according to the conversation in Acts 19:1-5, they were not aware of the Holy Spirit. The Apostle Paul knew the importance of the Holy Spirit, so he taught them about the Holy Spirit and laid hands upon them. Thereafter, they received the Holy Spirit (Acts 19:6).

There may be many believers today who have not heard of the Holy Spirit or have not experienced the Holy Spirit's power. However, those believers who have the Holy Spirit must allow the Holy Spirit to operate through their lives so that the world will see the power of God at work through his children.

Persons are sick and need healing. However, healing will not come through enticing words. Many times, medical professionals will try their best to help persons, but they may be unsuccessful in their efforts. However, through the Holy Spirit, healing will be made available. Through the Holy Spirit, demons will be driven off from those who are possessed. Therefore, those believers who do not have the Holy Spirit must go after God's Spirit.

Acts 19:1-12

1 And it came to pass, that, while Apollos was at Corinth, Paul having passed through the upper coasts came to Ephesus: and finding certain disciples, 2 He said unto them, Have ye received the Holy Ghost since ye believed? And they said unto him, We have not so much as heard whether there be any Holy Ghost. 3 And he said unto them, Unto what then were ye baptized? And they said, Unto John's baptism. 4 Then said Paul, John verily baptized with the baptism of repentance, saying unto the people, that they should believe on him which should come after him, that is, on Christ Jesus. 5 When they heard this, they were baptized in the name of the Lord Jesus. 6 And when Paul had laid his hands upon them, the Holy Ghost came on them; and they spake with tongues, and prophesied. 7 And all the men were about twelve.

8 And he went into the synagogue, and spake boldly for the space of three months, disputing and persuading the things concerning the kingdom of God. 9 But when divers were hardened, and believed not, but spake evil of that way before the multitude, he departed from them, and separated the disciples, disputing daily in the school of one Tyrannus. 10 And this continued by the space of two years; so that all they which dwelt in Asia heard the word of the Lord Jesus, both Jews and Greeks. 11 And God wrought special miracles by the hands of Paul: 12 So that from his body were brought unto the sick handkerchiefs or aprons, and the diseases departed from them, and the evil spirits went out of them.

10.1 Ordinary men transformed into powerful men

When Peter and John followed Jesus, they were ordinary men. They encountered struggles just like all other humans. However, when the Holy Spirit entered their lives, they were changed men. They had significant power, such that they were able to speak to a man who was begging at the gate of the temple called Beautiful, and he was healed.

When believers seek God, they can expect that he will empower them, and the things which seemed impossible to them in times past will be very simple for them to do, as the Holy Spirit will give them power.

Acts 3:1-9

1 Now Peter and John went up together into the temple at the hour of prayer, being the ninth hour. 2 And a certain man lame from his mother's womb was carried, whom they laid daily at the gate of the temple which is called Beautiful, to ask alms of them that entered into the temple; 3 Who seeing Peter and John about to go into the temple asked an alms. 4 And Peter, fastening his eyes upon him with John, said, Look on us. 5 And he gave heed unto them, expecting to receive something of them. 6 Then Peter said, Silver and gold have I none; but such as I have give I thee: In the name of Jesus Christ of Nazareth rise up and walk. 7 And he took him by the right hand, and lifted him up: and immediately his feet and ankle bones received strength. 8 And he leaping up stood, and walked, and entered with them into the temple, walking, and leaping, and praising God. 9 And all the people saw him walking and praising God.

Take note, Peter and John did not touch him, they just fastened their eyes on him (Acts 3:4). With the Holy Spirit on the lives of the believers, many great things will happen. Just imagine, if more believers go hard after God for his Spirit and exercise the power given to them through the Holy Spirit, then there will be many continuous testimonies of God's power.

11. Sinned, but not a sinner forever

Every human has sinned and will sin. No one is righteous.

11.1 No one is righteous

The Apostle Paul had the opportunity to talk to the believers and remind them that no one is righteous. This is a clear reminder that all have sinned and need Jesus to deliver them from their sins. It is important to see what Apostle Paul says to the Romans in Romans 3:9-20.

Romans 3:9-20

9 What then? are we better than they? No, in no wise: for we have before proved both Jews and Gentiles, that they are all under sin; 10 As it is written, There is none righteous, no, not one: 11 There is none that understandeth, there is none that seeketh after God. 12 They are all gone out of the way, they are together become unprofitable; there is none that doeth good, no, not one. 13 Their throat is an open sepulchre; with their tongues they have used deceit; the poison of asps is under their lips: 14 Whose mouth is full of cursing and bitterness: 15 Their feet are swift to shed blood: 16 Destruction and misery are in their ways: 17 And the way of peace have they not known: 18 There is no fear of God before their eyes. 19 Now we know that what things soever the law saith, it saith to them who are under the law: that every mouth may be stopped, and all the world may become guilty before God. 20 Therefore by the deeds of the law there shall no flesh be justified in his sight: for by the law is the knowledge of sin.

Many of the Romans followed the laws. However, as they followed the laws, they did not fulfill all of the requirements of God and they missed the mark on many occasions. Apostle Paul wanted to help them to move away from the laws and to follow Jesus, so that their sins will be forgiven and that they will have hope of his saving grace.

11.2 King David sinned but sought forgiveness

The story of King David's sin is known to many persons. However, many persons have not placed much emphasis on the fact that David went hard after God, for God to forgive him of his sins so that his relationship with the Lord would be restored. King David had seen the mighty hand of God working in and through his life. He knew that after he sinned, he did not enjoy the presence and power of God. He also knew that without God, he would lose many of his battles as a warrior.

If many persons would recognize that they are not having the victories which the Lord promised, then they will know it is time for them to seek more of God. A beautiful thing about the Lord is that he is willing to forgive sins.

King David knew that if his sins were to be forgiven, then he must take personal responsibility to go after God. The king recognized that his status could not save him, so he went to God. When some persons sin, they are trying to take many different directions for their sins to be forgiven. However, all those who have sinned and need forgiveness must come to the Lord, since people cannot forgive sins.

Psalm 51:1-19

¹ Have mercy upon me, O God, according to thy lovingkindness: according unto the multitude of thy tender mercies blot out my transgressions. ² Wash me throughly from mine iniquity, and cleanse me from my sin. ³ For I acknowledge my transgressions: and my sin is ever before me. ⁴ Against thee, thee only, have I sinned, and done this evil in thy sight: that thou mightest be justified when thou speakest, and be clear when thou judgest. ⁵ Behold, I was shapen in iniquity; and in sin did my mother conceive me. ⁶ Behold, thou desirest truth in the inward parts: and in the hidden part thou shalt make me to know wisdom. ⁷ Purge me with hyssop, and I shall be clean: wash me, and I shall be whiter than snow. ⁸ Make me to hear joy and gladness; that the bones which thou hast broken may rejoice. ⁹ Hide thy face from my sins, and blot out all mine iniquities. ¹⁰ Create in me a clean heart, O God; and renew a right spirit within me. ¹¹ Cast me not away from thy presence; and take not thy holy spirit from me. ¹² Restore unto me the joy of thy salvation; and uphold me with thy free spirit. ¹³ Then will I teach transgressors thy ways; and sinners shall be converted unto thee. ¹⁴ Deliver me from bloodguiltiness, O God, thou God of my salvation: and my tongue shall sing aloud of thy righteousness. ¹⁵ O Lord, open thou my lips; and my mouth shall shew forth thy praise. ¹⁶ For thou desirest not sacrifice; else would I give it:

thou delightest not in burnt offering. 17 The sacrifices of God are a broken spirit: a broken and a contrite heart, O God, thou wilt not despise. 18 Do good in thy good pleasure unto Zion: build thou the walls of Jerusalem. 19 Then shalt thou be pleased with the sacrifices of righteousness, with burnt offering and whole burnt offering: then shall they offer bullocks upon thine altar.

Figure 10. King David's actions after he sinned (Psalm 51:1-19)

He knew that he sinned (v. 2)

He went to God concerning his sins (v. 1)

If sins are not forgiven, then those sins are always present (v. 3)

He acknowledged that he sinned against God (v. 4)

When persons are born, they are born in sin (v. 5)

God always requires truthfulness with everyone (v. 6)

David wanted God to remove his sins (v. 8-9)

David wanted God to renew his spirit, since it is through God's spirit that he encountered victories (v. 10-12)

After David was restored, he wanted to teach persons about God and worship (v. 13-15)

God cannot be bribed, but needs persons to seek forgiveness (v. 16-19)

Take note, David was king. When he sinned, he knew that his relationship with God was affected. Without God's presence, he would have not been a great leader. With all this in mind, David went to God and poured out his heart, so that his relationship with God would be restored.

12. Helping a friend to be healed

Do you have many good friends who are willing to do anything to help you to be healed? Or, if the question was to be reversed, do you have any good friends who you are willing to do anything to help to be healed?

12.1 Many friends, but few good friends

In life, everyone expects to have friends. While some persons prefer to be alone, they still need friends. However, not everyone will have many good friends. Good friendship is not easy to establish and maintain. There are not many friends who are willing to do whatever it takes to help others. It is often seen that when some persons have a great need for help, no one is available and willing to help them.

Persons will become sick from time to time. Sometimes, the sickness of a person is because of their negligence. However, there are times when persons become sick despite following most of the medical practitioner's advice.

Luke 5:17-26

17 And it came to pass on a certain day, as he was teaching, that there were Pharisees and doctors of the law sitting by, which were come out of every town of Galilee, and Judaea, and Jerusalem: and the power of the Lord was present to heal them. 18 And, behold, men brought in a bed a man which was taken with a palsy: and they sought means to bring him in, and to lay him before him. 19 And when they could not find by what way they might bring him in because of the multitude, they went upon the housetop, and let him down through the tiling with his couch into the midst before Jesus. 20 And when he saw their faith, he said unto him, Man, thy sins are forgiven thee.

21 And the scribes and the Pharisees began to reason, saying, Who is this which speaketh blasphemies? Who can forgive sins, but God alone? 22 But when Jesus perceived their thoughts, he answering said unto them, What reason ye in your hearts? 23 Whether is easier, to say, Thy sins be forgiven thee; or to say, Rise up and walk? 24 But that ye may know that the Son of man hath power upon earth to forgive sins, (he said unto the sick of the palsy,) I say unto thee, Arise, and take up thy couch, and go into thine house. 25 And immediately he rose up before them, and took up that whereon he lay, and departed to his own house, glorifying God. 26 And they were all amazed, and they glorified God, and were filled with fear, saying, We have seen strange things to day.

The courage of these friends must be commended. They knew that Jesus was having a meeting with others in a building. There were many dignitaries in the building, so they knew that it was going to be difficult to get Jesus' attention. These men never asked who owned the building and what would be the cost of any damages they may cause. The only focus on these friends' minds was to take the sick man before Jesus so that he would be healed. Their faith moved Jesus, and Jesus healed their friend.

Some persons are sick today, and if their good friends care about them, then they should take action to help those who have a great need for healing. There are some friends who will spend a lot of money in seeking for their friend to be healed. However, more people need to do more to help other persons in receiving their healing and blessings.

God wants persons to go hard after him. The faith demonstrated by these friends was sufficient to gain the attention of Jesus, and their friend was healed because of their actions. Some persons try to impress others about what good friends they are with others. However, those who demonstrate their friendship through actions are often good friends to cherish.

13. Seek quality mentors

When God calls persons to serve him, he expects that they are willing to work along with others. The work of the Lord cannot be completed by one individual. Therefore, there is always a need for many persons to join in doing God's work.

When a person joins the body of Christ, they will need much guidance. The guidance they are expected to receive will help them to be effective and efficient for the work of the Lord. Persons who lack experience concerning the things of God may spend much time frustrating themselves, and if they become frustrated, they may soon quit.

13.1 Elijah placed his cloak on Elisha

Elisha the servant of God was ploughing the field with some oxen. God used Elijah to visit him in the field and to place the cloak on him. Immediately after the cloak was placed on Elisha, he knew that God had called him to ministry.

How many persons today feel the presence of God in their lives but are still doing what they were doing before? When God places his presence upon an individual, he wants them to know that it is time for them to work for him. Each person's work will be different, but God wants everyone to work for him.

1 Kings 19:19-21

19 So he departed thence and found Elisha the son of Shaphat, who was plowing with twelve yoke of oxen before him, and he with the twelfth: and Elijah passed by him, and cast his mantle upon him. 20 And he left the oxen, and ran after Elijah, and said, Let me, I pray thee, kiss my father and my mother, and then I will follow thee. And he said unto him, Go back again: for what have I done to thee? 21 And he returned back from him, and took a yoke of oxen, and slew them, and boiled their flesh with the instruments of the oxen, and gave unto the people, and they did eat. Then he arose, and went after Elijah, and ministered unto him.

To be called by God is one thing, but not many persons can subject themselves to be mentored. After some persons have received the anointing of God, they feel that they can operate without the wisdom of others who are working for the Lord.

"Mentoring and coaching are similar approaches in that they are both about one individual (coach or mentor) helping another. In common language, we may even equate the two, but there are important differences. A mentor is usually someone who has particular relevant experience, knowledge, or skills, and maybe more senior than the person being mentored. The relationship is often specific to a period of transition as someone enters a new role or takes on new responsibilities that are within the mentor's own experience" (Nicholas and Baker, 2013).

The mentor must be willing to help the protégé, and the protégé must be willing to work along with the mentor. It is seen that Elisha was willing to follow his mentor.

Within the relationship, the mentor generally fills one or more of the following four leading roles:

Figure 11. Main roles of the mentor

(Developed from Shields et al., 2016)

Each protégé must know that the mentor has some main roles, but is not there to do everything for them. However, the protégé must be prepared to follow the advice of the mentor if they want to become successful.

13.2 Elijah mentored Elisha

Elisha knew that he needed to work with Elijah, as he would gain much experience. Elijah accepted the responsibility to work with his protégé.

The relationship between Elijah and Elisha blossomed, and they went from place to place together. As Elijah went hard after God, Elisha was able to experience many of these events and knew that he should follow a similar pattern.

Elijah was not a leader who was looking to be famous. He was concerned about doing the works which the Lord had called him to do.

Many protégés need mentors who are not looking for the applause of men, but willing to go hard after God. The Lord is looking for more protégés like Elisha who are willing to go hard after him, no matter what it will cost them.

When Elisha followed his mentor, it was not an easy thing, but he knew what he wanted from God. There were many distractions as Elisha followed Elijah, but Elisha did not give up. He knew that he needed something from God, and no one was going to stop him from reaching what God can do for him.

2 Kings 2:2-15

2 And Elijah said unto Elisha, Tarry here, I pray thee; for the LORD hath sent me to Bethel. And Elisha said unto him, As the LORD liveth, and as thy soul liveth, I will not leave thee. So they went down to Bethel. 3 And the sons of the prophets that were at Bethel came forth to Elisha, and said unto him, Knowest thou that the LORD will take away thy master from thy head to day? And he said, Yea, I know it; hold ye your peace. 4 And Elijah said unto him, Elisha, tarry here, I pray thee; for the LORD hath sent me to Jericho. And he said, As the LORD liveth, and as thy soul liveth, I will not leave thee. So they came to Jericho.

5 And the sons of the prophets that were at Jericho came to Elisha, and said unto him, Knowest thou that the LORD will take away thy master from thy head to day? And he answered, Yea, I know it; hold ye your peace. 6 And Elijah said unto him, Tarry, I pray thee, here; for the LORD hath sent me to Jordan. And he said, As the LORD liveth, and as thy soul liveth, I will not leave thee. And they two went on.

⁷And fifty men of the sons of the prophets went, and stood to view afar off: and they two stood by Jordan. ⁸And Elijah took his mantle, and wrapped it together, and smote the waters, and they were divided hither and thither, so that they two went over on dry ground. ⁹And it came to pass, when they were gone over, that Elijah said unto Elisha, Ask what I shall do for thee, before I be taken away from thee. And Elisha said, I pray thee, let a double portion of thy spirit be upon me. ¹⁰And he said, Thou hast asked a hard thing: nevertheless, if thou see me when I am taken from thee, it shall be so unto thee; but if not, it shall not be so. ¹¹And it came to pass, as they still went on, and talked, that, behold, there appeared a chariot of fire, and horses of fire, and parted them both asunder; and Elijah went up by a whirlwind into heaven. ¹²And Elisha saw it, and he cried, My father, my father, the chariot of Israel, and the horsemen thereof. And he saw him no more: and he took hold of his own clothes, and rent them in two pieces. ¹³He took up also the mantle of Elijah that fell from him, and went back, and stood by the bank of Jordan; ¹⁴And he took the mantle of Elijah that fell from him, and smote the waters, and said, Where is the LORD God of Elijah? and when he also had smitten the waters, they parted hither and thither: and Elisha went over. ¹⁵And when the sons of the prophets which were to view at Jericho saw him, they said, The spirit of Elijah doth rest on Elisha. And they came to meet him, and bowed themselves to the ground before him.

As they both journeyed, Elijah spoke with Elisha. During their conversation and their walking, Elisha ought to have learned many things.

Many persons must take the opportunity when they communicate with great leaders to learn many things from them. No great leader will live forever, so whatever there is to learn, learn it very early.

13.3 Do not stop until you are empowered

Elijah knew that the Lord was bringing his ministry on earth to an end. Therefore, on several occasions, Elijah shared with Elisha that he did not need to continue the journey. However, Elisha understood that if he was going to be effective for God, then he had to be empowered. He pressed on and followed Elijah.

"As the LORD liveth, and as thy soul liveth, I will not leave thee." This became the common response from Elisha, as he planned to stay with his mentor until he received great power from God.

It will be good to see many mentee being hungry for God, where they are willing to follow their mentor until they receive their blessings. Elisha did not only follow his mentor, but he received that which he had asked God to do for him.

14. Touching his garment is enough

During Jesus' earthly ministry, many persons listened to him. They would stop what they were doing and give great attention to his teaching.

However, there was a woman who had a medical condition which the physicians could not remedy. She tried several physicians and spent all of her monies, but her condition did not improve. It can be frustrating to spend all of your money and find that no one can help you.

When many persons are sick for even one day, they feel uncomfortable. However, this woman's medical condition was not for one day, but twelve long years. This is a very long time for anyone to be sick.

Luke 8:43-48

43 And a woman having an issue of blood twelve years, which had spent all her living upon physicians, neither could be healed of any, 44 Came behind him, and touched the border of his garment: and immediately her issue of blood stanched. 45 And Jesus said, Who touched me? When all denied, Peter and they that were with him said, Master, the multitude throng thee and press thee, and sayest thou, Who touched me? 46 And Jesus said, Somebody hath touched me: for I perceive that virtue is gone out of me. 47 And when the woman saw that she was not hid, she came trembling, and falling down before him, she declared unto him before all the people for what cause she had touched him, and how she was healed immediately. 48 And he said unto her, Daughter, be of good comfort: thy faith hath made thee whole; go in peace.

While this story about the woman with the issue of blood has been preached many times, it is still worth discussing. There are three main areas to discuss about this woman's action:

- Know what you need
- Know who can meet your needs
- Go passionately after your needs

14.1 Know what you need

Every believer has needs, but not every believer will announce those needs to the world. Some persons are afraid to let others know that they have needs because they feel persons will laugh at them. Firstly, if anyone must come to Christ, they must believe that he is a rewarder to those who diligently seek him (Hebrews 11:6). The size of your need is never a distraction for the Lord (Matthew 7:7-8).

14.2 Know who can meet your needs

Not many persons can and will help you. Therefore, you have to know who can help you. In Luke 8:43-48, this woman went to several physicians for help (v. 43). These physicians tried to assist her, but they were unsuccessful. Even so, she had to pay for medical service whenever she visited the physicians (v. 43).

After twelve years of visiting various physicians, she decided to try Jesus. It meant that she was constantly listening out for any new ways for her health to be restored. She was not willing to give up; she was pressing towards her success.

14.3 Go passionately after your needs

Are there believers who still have a need and believe that Jesus can meet that need? This woman had many challenges to overcome to touch Jesus. It was not normal for women to get very close to Jesus. Many men were surrounding Jesus, which made it difficult to have direct access to him, and many of those persons were in better health than she was.

Persons who believe God is a healer must passionately follow after the Lord as their great help. If they need help, then these are the things they must do:

- Identify their need (v. 43).
- Follow their dream (v. 43)
- Seek for those who can help them (v. 43)
- Ignore the naysayers (v. 45)
- Press towards their dream (v. 43)
- Testify openly about their healing (v. 47)

Jesus always knows when someone has touched him, since it makes a difference in the kingdom (Luke 8:46). He is willing to meet all of their needs

(Matthew 6: 33). The scripture never mentions this woman's name, but it does mention her action. No one knew how many attempts she made to touch him, but everyone knew that she touched his garment. Believers have to go hard after God if they need something from him, especially this year. He is waiting for believers to touch him.

When people cannot help you, then keep your eyes on Jesus for your help (Psalm 121:1-3). In this season in your life, you may have many challenges, but with God, you will be successful, if you only allow him to be the master over your life. You must press hard towards doing the things of the Lord, as the Lord will reward his children (Psalm 68:19). Jesus will not turn you away when you come to him for help, since your faith moves the Lord (Luke 8:48).

After examining this woman's action, it is clear that everyone can take an example from her. She did not allow people or things to distract her. She was willing to touch Jesus.

If there is anyone who wants to go hard after God, then they have to keep their eyes focused and go to Jesus as their healer. Sometimes, there may be friends and family members who will be there to distract those who have a need, but they must remain resolute and seek God for their blessings.

15. Blind, but needing sight

Some persons with physical ailments have accepted that life will not change. Those persons who have physical sight must always be thankful, since there are many persons who are unable to see. Those who want their sight to be restored may visit the optician or optometrist in an effort to ensure that they are restored with sight.

Mark 10:46-52

46 And they came to Jericho: and as he went out of Jericho with his disciples and a great number of people, blind Bartimaeus, the son of Timaeus, sat by the highway side begging. 47 And when he heard that it was Jesus of Nazareth, he began to cry out, and say, Jesus, thou son of David, have mercy on me. 48 And many charged him that he should hold his peace: but he cried the more a great deal, Thou son of David, have mercy on me. 49 And Jesus stood still, and commanded him to be called. And they call the blind man, saying unto him, Be of good comfort, rise; he calleth thee. 50 And he, casting away his garment, rose, and came to Jesus. 51 And Jesus answered and said unto him, What wilt thou that I should do unto thee? The blind man said unto him, Lord, that I might receive my sight. 52 And Jesus said unto him, Go thy way; thy faith hath made thee whole. And immediately he received his sight, and followed Jesus in the way.

Figure 12. Events for Bartimaeus' sight to be restored (Mark 10:46-52)

- He heard or recognized that Jesus was passing by (v. 47)
- He cried out to Jesus on the first occassion (v. 47)
- He acknowledged that Jesus is the son of David (v. 47)
- He asked Jesus to have mercy on him (v. 47)
- The crowd asked him to be quiet, but he cried louder for Jesus to have mercy on him (v. 48)
- Jesus stood still (v. 49)
- Jesus commanded the people to call Bartimaeus to come to him (v. 49)
- The people followed Jesus' instruction and called Bartimaeus (v. 49)
- The people motivated Bartimaeus and told him to be of good courage (v. 49)
- Bartimaeus cast away his garment (v. 50)
- Bartimaeus rose up from his position (v. 50)
- Bartimaeus walked towards Jesus despite being blind (v. 50)
- Jesus asked Bartimaeus, "What wilt thou that I should do unto thee?" (v. 51)
- The blind man knew what he wanted and immediately told Jesus that he needed his sight (v. 51)
- Jesus said unto Bartimaeus, "Go thy way; thy faith hath made thee whole" (v. 52)
- Bartimaeus immediately received his sight (v. 52)
- Bartimaeus followed Jesus (v. 52)

In every country, some persons are blind. However, take note that in Mark 10:46-52, Bartimaeus was blind, but he was not going to accept blindness forever. He needed his sight, and he needed it today.

Many persons are unsure of what they need. They are not specific about their needs, and they do not know when they need their healing. But Bartimaeus knew what he needed and when he needed it.

Jesus was and is still looking for some persons to go hard after him. The faith of Bartimaeus moved Jesus, and Jesus immediately connected with him. Jesus reminded Bartimaeus that it was his faith that contributed to his healing.

Many persons want Jesus to heal them, but they do not want to exercise any faith. The hands of God are often outstretched to meet the needs of many persons, but not all of these persons are reaching out to him. Today, if you need something from Jesus, reach out to him and call him. While the people wanted Bartimaeus to be quiet (Mark 10:48), he ignored their request and cried louder to Jesus.

Bartimaeus knew that only Jesus was able to heal him. He was not crying for the crowd's support; he was crying to Jesus to give him sight. If every believer goes hard after God for their needs, they can be assured that God will listen to them and deliver them. Jesus eventually stopped what he was doing because Bartimaeus was crying louder and needed the healing hands of God. After Jesus healed Bartimaeus, there was no need for Bartimaeus to disturb the people with his loud noise.

16. The Canaanite woman pressed Jesus to heal her daughter

People are sometimes physically sick and visit physicians for healing. But when persons are possessed by demons, then they need the healing hands of Jesus.

In Matthew 15:22-29, we read that the Canaanite woman's daughter was demon-possessed. As a caring mother, she wanted her daughter to be healed. So, she went to Jesus, knowing that he would be the delivery. In her salutation, she referred to him as a son of David. While Jesus heard the woman's plea, he did not immediately respond to her. The disciples felt that Jesus did not want anything to do with this Canaanite woman. However, this woman was not willing to take no for an answer. She continued to press until she got Jesus to respond to her.

Matthew 15:22-29

22 And, behold, a woman of Canaan came out of the same coasts, and cried unto him, saying, Have mercy on me, O Lord, thou son of David; my daughter is grievously vexed with a devil. 23 But he answered her not a word. And his disciples came and besought him, saying, Send her away; for she crieth after us. 24 But he answered and said, I am not sent but unto the lost sheep of the house of Israel. 25 Then came she and worshipped him, saying, Lord, help me. 26 But he answered and said, It is not meet to take the children's bread, and to cast it to dogs. 27 And she said, Truth, Lord: yet the dogs eat of the crumbs which fall from their masters' table. 28 Then Jesus answered and said unto her, O woman, great is thy faith: be it unto thee even as thou wilt. And her daughter was made whole from that very hour. 29 And Jesus departed from thence, and came nigh unto the sea of Galilee; and went up into a mountain, and sat down there.

Figure 13. Events between the Canaanite woman and Jesus (Matthew 15:22-29)

The Canaanite woman left where she was to come and meet Jesus (v. 22)

She cried unto Jesus (v. 22)

She told Jesus that her daughter needed deliverance (v. 22)

Jesus did not answer her on her first plea (v. 23)

Jesus' disciples asked Jesus to send the Canaanite woman away (v. 23)

The Canaanite woman approached Jesus again (v. 25)

On her second communication with Jesus, she worshipped him (v. 25)

Jesus answered her on the second occasion (v. 26)

Jesus' response to her was demotivating (v. 26)

She had a positive response to Jesus' demotivating statement (v. 27)

Jesus answered her again; she had touched his emotion (v. 28)

Jesus acknowledged her great faith (v. 28)

Her daughter was healed and delivered immediately (v. 28)

On the first occasion when she approached Jesus, he did not acknowledge her statement, nor her presence. However, she was persistent, and as she stayed within his sight, she got his attention. While Jesus spoke to her harshly, she did not run away and cry. She immediately provided him with a positive response.

Too many believers are willing to run away from the presence of the Lord if he remains silent to their first request. Many times, the Lord wants to see how hungry his children are for whatever they approach him about. God wants to do many things for his children, but he wants them to ask.

Matthew 7:7-8

[7] Ask, and it shall be given you; seek, and ye shall find; knock, and it shall be opened unto you: [8] For every one that asketh receiveth; and he that seeketh findeth; and to him that knocketh it shall be opened.

When one examines Matthew 7:7-8, they will recognize that God wants his children to be zealous as they approach him. Those believers who are lackadaisical will not get anything from God.

Figure 14. Intensify your effort to seek God for your blessing (Matthew 7:7-8)

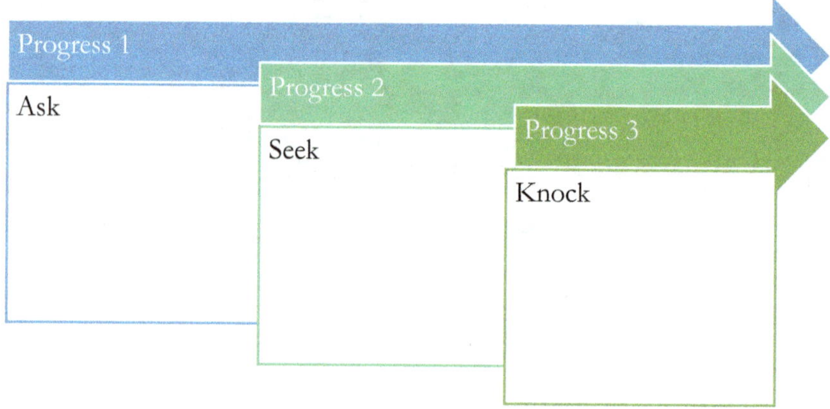

If the Canaanite woman had turned away on the first occasion, then her daughter would have remained demon-possessed. The Canaanites were not entitled to certain blessings. However, the woman understood that but knew that while it was not her right, she was not going to leave him until she was blessed.

Similarly, when some persons attend a job interview, they are afraid that they failed based upon the questions that were asked, but other interviewees show that they are willing to put in their best effort for the job. Some leave the room without any hope, but many interviewers want to see applicants with a fighting spirit. They want to know that the applicants they are about to employ have tenacity. It is a similar thing for the kingdom of God.

Whenever persons gave their lives to Christ, they must be have an attitude where they are not willing to give up on their faith. They must not quit concerning the promises of God for their lives. While there will always be obstacles in the way of believers, they must go hard after God until he helps them to cross those obstacles.

God wants to be with his children all the way. He knows that his children will have to go through fire and flood, but he will be there for them. That is a caring God.

Isaiah 43:2-3

2 When thou passest through the waters, I will be with thee; and through the rivers, they shall not overflow thee: when thou walkest through the fire, thou shalt not be burned; neither shall the flame kindle upon thee. 3 For I am the LORD thy God, the Holy One of Israel, thy Saviour: I gave Egypt for thy ransom, Ethiopia and Seba for thee.

During the time of the fires and the floods, the Lord will be there for those believers who place him first in their lives. The floods and fires can destroy people, but when God is there with his children, neither the fires nor the floods will destroy them.

17. Bless me before you go

The life of Jacob is one of a man who did many wrong things. The relationship between Jacob and his brother Esau was strained. Despite both of them being children from the same parents, they had their struggles, and their struggles continued into their adult lives. Nevertheless, Jacob wanted to approach his brother and reconcile, so he brought his family and his servants with him to see Esau.

On his way, Jacob had already planned his strategies for how he would approach his brother. He had some presents to give to his brother and was hoping that that would help to create some peace between them. However, Jacob was afraid that Esau would kill him. Fear had gripped his heart, and he did not want to be smitten.

Genesis 32:11

11 Deliver me, I pray thee, from the hand of my brother, from the hand of Esau: for I fear him, lest he will come and smite me, and the mother with the children.

It is often amazing that people who do bad things do not want anyone to do bad things to them, nor do they want to die. As Jacob was on his way to reconcile with his brother, an angel from the Lord met him, and he called the place Mahanaim, according to Genesis 32:2.

17.1 Wanting to reconcile

When some persons become older, they want to put aside all the bad things they have done and reconcile with those whom they hurt. Many children did bad things to their parents. As some of those children become mature and have their own children, they realize that they have lived a good life with their parents, so they will seek to reconcile their relationships with their parents. Some parents also have to reconcile with their children.

Jacob was desperate to make his relationship right with his brother. He was not sure what the outcome would be, since he had done many bad things to his brother, but he was willing to approach his brother and reconcile his relationship.

The angel of God met Jacob on his way as he was going to reconcile with his brother. Jacob had a conversation with the angel and explained why he was going to meet his brother. The servants of Jacob went before him, carrying presents to Esau.

Jacob told his servants that when they meet Esau and he asks them about the presents they brought, they must mention his name. He also told them to let Esau know that Jacob was on his way to meet him. It is seen that Jacob had his plan well organized as he wanted to have a better relationship with his brother.

As Jacob sent his servants with presents to meet his brother, he was hoping that his brother would accept the presents and that peace would prevail. Jacob was smart in his thinking, and he hoped that the servants he sent to meet his brother would return to him with the good news that Esau accepted the presents.

17.2 Tired after a long journey

After traveling a long distance, Jacob was tired. As a person grows older, they do not always have the strength to walk the same distance as when they were younger. Many children wonder how the same parents who had once walked long distances are now unable to walk those same distances within a short time. As some persons age, their wisdom increases, but their physical strength may fail.

The distance to reach Esau was very long. Jacob rested, then woke up in the night and continued his journey (Genesis 32:22). Once there is enough visibility, the person who has to walk long distances may enjoy it more when the weather is cool. Oftentimes, when the sun is out and it becomes hot, persons become tired, and they may do less compared to what they would do in cooler temperatures.

17.3 Jacob demanded a blessing from the angel

The life of Jacob shows that he loved to fight. He was willing to take on a challenge and hoped that he was going to be successful. As Jacob was on his way to meet Esau, he sent his family members before him, so he was eventually alone (Genesis 32:24).

As Jacob was alone, he wrestled with the angel. This appears to be a strange story, since never before had anyone wrestled with an angel. Not only did Jacob wrestle with the angel during the night, but according to the scriptures, the battle was intense and Jacob was not willing to give up. It appears that Jacob either had an advantage as they wrestled or both of them were equal in the battle (Genesis 32:25).

Figure 15. What happened when Jacob wrestled with the angel?

What is also interesting about this scripture is that Jacob was not willing to let the angel go until he was blessed. Every believer must have such a passion that they need God to bless them and will not let that moment pass them.

Many believers are too reserved in their approach as they serve God. While God has promised them many things, they operate as though they are not entitled to the blessings of God.

If more believers take on an approach like Jacob, as told in Genesis 32:26, they will have many of the things which God has promised. Jacob was clear in his communication as he wrestled with the angel. The battle between Jacob and the angel occurred between the night and the breaking of the day, and Jacob was not going to let the angel depart until he received a blessing. He knew that once he was blessed, he would be able to face many challenges and be victorious.

No believer must be comfortable with an ordinary life. They must be willing to go hard after God until he blesses them. Without the blessing of God, believers will be living below God's standard. Jacob knew that when the night was over, he must be blessed, and he sought his blessing.

Genesis 32:1-32

¹ And Jacob went on his way, and the angels of God met him. ² And when Jacob saw them, he said, This is God's host: and he called the name of that place Mahanaim. ³ And Jacob sent messengers before him to Esau his brother unto the land of Seir, the country of Edom. ⁴ And he commanded them, saying, Thus shall ye speak unto my lord Esau; Thy servant Jacob saith thus, I have sojourned with Laban, and stayed there until now: ⁵ And I have oxen, and asses, flocks, and menservants, and womenservants: and I have sent to tell my lord, that I may find grace in thy sight. ⁶ And the messengers returned to Jacob, saying, We came to thy brother Esau, and also he cometh to meet thee, and four hundred men with him. ⁷ Then Jacob was greatly afraid and distressed: and he divided the people that was with him, and the flocks, and herds, and the camels, into two bands; ⁸ And said, If Esau come to the one company, and smite it, then the other company which is left shall escape.

⁹ And Jacob said, O God of my father Abraham, and God of my father Isaac, the LORD which saidst unto me, Return unto thy country, and to thy kindred, and I will deal well with thee: ¹⁰ I am not worthy of the least of all the mercies, and of all the truth, which thou hast shewed unto thy servant; for with my staff I passed over this Jordan; and now I am become two bands. ¹¹ Deliver me, I pray thee, from the hand of my brother, from the hand of Esau: for I fear him, lest he will come and smite me, and the mother with the children. 12 And thou saidst, I will surely do thee good, and make thy seed as the sand of the sea, which cannot be numbered for multitude.

13 And he lodged there that same night; and took of that which came to his hand a present for Esau his brother; 14 Two hundred she goats, and twenty he goats, two hundred ewes, and twenty rams, 15 Thirty milch camels with their colts, forty kine, and ten bulls, twenty she asses, and ten foals. 16 And he delivered them into the hand of his servants, every drove by themselves; and said unto his servants, Pass over before me, and put a space betwixt drove and drove. 17 And he commanded the foremost, saying, When Esau my brother meeteth thee, and asketh thee, saying, Whose art thou? and whither goest thou? and whose are these before thee? 18 Then thou shalt say, They be thy servant Jacob's; it is a present sent unto my lord Esau: and, behold, also he is behind us. 19 And so commanded he the second, and the third, and all that followed the droves, saying, On this manner shall ye speak unto Esau, when ye find him. 20 And say ye moreover, Behold, thy servant Jacob is behind us. For he said, I will appease him with the present that goeth before me, and afterward I will see his face; peradventure he will accept of me. 21 So went the present over before him: and himself lodged that night in the company. 22 And he rose up that night, and took his two wives, and his two womenservants, and his eleven sons, and passed over the ford Jabbok. 23 And he took them, and sent them over the brook, and sent over that he had. 24 And Jacob was left alone; and there wrestled a man with him until the breaking of the day. 25 And when he saw that he prevailed not against him, he touched the hollow of his thigh; and the hollow of Jacob's thigh was out of joint, as he wrestled with him. 26 And he said, Let me go, for the day breaketh. And he said, I will not let thee go, except thou bless me. 27 And he said unto him, What is thy name? And he said, Jacob. 28 And he said, Thy name shall be called no more Jacob, but Israel: for as a prince hast thou power with God and with men, and hast prevailed. 29 And Jacob asked him, and said, Tell me, I pray thee, thy name. And he said, Wherefore is it that thou dost ask after my name? And he blessed him there. 30 And Jacob called the name of the place Peniel: for I have seen God face to face, and my life is preserved. 31 And as he passed over Penuel the sun rose upon him, and he halted upon his thigh. 32 Therefore the children of Israel eat not of the sinew which shrank, which is upon the hollow of the thigh, unto this day: because he touched the hollow of Jacob's thigh in the sinew that shrank.

17.4 Jacob's name changed

While Jacob was known for so many bad things, he was still willing to seek a blessing. Can believers adopt a similar approach, knowing that God has promised them many good things and continuing to seek God until he changes them?

After the battle, Jacob's thigh was disjointed. However, his name has changed, and to this day, the name of the place remains. Jacob had a bad history, but he was not going to let his past distract him from what God had in store for him.

Since Jacob demanded a blessing and he received it, then believers must know what God has promised them, and they must constantly seek God until he gives it to them. The name of Jacob changed and he was given a new name: Israel.

When persons walk with God, they must have something to show others that God has blessed them and they are not the same person as they were many years ago, before they were saved. There are so many blessings which God has for these children, but he wants them to demand their blessing. He does not want them to wait until tomorrow to demand their blessings; they must demand their blessing right now. There is no need to procrastinate in seeking God for his blessing today. If Jacob had allowed the angel to depart, then there might have not been any history of Israel, and his brother might have smitten him.

Jesus reminded all believers to ask God for their daily needs, according to Matthew 6:9-15. He also reminded them that they must ask God for whatever they need.

Matthew 7:7-8

7 Ask, and it shall be given you; seek, and ye shall find; knock, and it shall be opened unto you: 8 For every one that asketh receiveth; and he that seeketh findeth; and to him that knocketh it shall be opened.

Jacob went hard after God. He fought with the angel. His name was changed, and he was a different man because of the blessing of the Lord upon his life.

18. Unless God goes with you, do not go

Many persons believe that they are strong and wise enough by themselves and that they do not need God. But without the presence of God, believers are unable to have any impact.

Many persons are having defeat after defeat, not recognizing that they lack the presence of God, thus resulting in their life not making an impact.

18.1 God was angry with the children of Israel

The children of Israel had many opportunities and challenges. As God led them through his servant Moses, they did some things which were not pleasing to God. God was so displeased with their actions and attitude that he said to Moses that these children are "stiff-necked."

For any parent to call their children stiff-necked means that those children have done something which angers their parents. The behavior of the children of Israel made it very challenging for Moses to lead them.

Take note, Moses was leading the people of God, and God was displeased with them. Then the question is, where do we go from here? Moses was depending on God for direction, but God was not satisfied with them, so Moses was not sure what the next move should be.

18.2 Moses demanded to see God's glory

While God was angry with the children of Israel for their stiff-necked behavior, Moses wanted God to show him his glory before continuing to lead the children of Israel. It is seen that Moses was pressing God to do something important. He took an action that many believers need to do. They must go hard after God until God shows them his glory. Believers must not move from one location to another until they are assured that the Lord is going with them.

One of the reasons why many believers find themselves in defeat is that they are moving ahead of God. After Moses and the children of Israel settled on Mount Horeb, God asked them to strip themselves of their ornaments. Sometimes, people have too many things which are distracting them from hearing and receiving from God. Some persons have so many distractions around their lives that they spend less time with God.

While God hovered over the tent that Moses was in, Moses still wanted God to show him his glory. The people saw the cloudy pillar, but Moses needed more than that if he was going to continue to lead God's people. Moses therefore demanded that God show him his glory (Exodus 33:14-17).

Some persons may believe that Moses was too harsh on God. However, Moses was in a difficult situation. He had to lead the people of God, but the people of God were stiff-necked and God was displeased with their actions and attitude. Moses needed to know what to do next.

Exodus 33:1-23

1 And the LORD said unto Moses, Depart, and go up hence, thou and the people which thou hast brought up out of the land of Egypt, unto the land which I sware unto Abraham, to Isaac, and to Jacob, saying, Unto thy seed will I give it: 2 And I will send an angel before thee; and I will drive out the Canaanite, the Amorite, and the Hittite, and the Perizzite, the Hivite, and the Jebusite: 3 Unto a land flowing with milk and honey: for I will not go up in the midst of thee; for thou art a stiffnecked people: lest I consume thee in the way. 4 And when the people heard these evil tidings, they mourned: and no man did put on him his ornaments. 5 For the LORD had said unto Moses, Say unto the children of Israel, Ye are a stiffnecked people: I will come up into the midst of thee in a moment, and consume thee: therefore now put off thy ornaments from thee, that I may know what to do unto thee. 6 And the children of Israel stripped themselves of their ornaments by the mount Horeb.

7 And Moses took the tabernacle, and pitched it without the camp, afar off from the camp, and called it the Tabernacle of the congregation. And it came to pass, that every one which sought the LORD went out unto the tabernacle of the congregation, which was without the camp. 8 And it came to pass, when Moses went out unto the tabernacle, that all the people rose up, and stood every man at his tent door, and looked after Moses, until he was gone into the tabernacle. 9 And it came to pass, as Moses entered into the tabernacle, the cloudy pillar descended, and stood at the door of the tabernacle, and the Lord talked with

Moses. ¹⁰ And all the people saw the cloudy pillar stand at the tabernacle door: and all the people rose up and worshipped, every man in his tent door.

¹¹ And the LORD spake unto Moses face to face, as a man speaketh unto his friend. And he turned again into the camp: but his servant Joshua, the son of Nun, a young man, departed not out of the tabernacle. ¹² And Moses said unto the LORD, See, thou sayest unto me, Bring up this people: and thou hast not let me know whom thou wilt send with me. Yet thou hast said, I know thee by name, and thou hast also found grace in my sight. ¹³ Now therefore, I pray thee, if I have found grace in thy sight, shew me now thy way, that I may know thee, that I may find grace in thy sight: and consider that this nation is thy people. ¹⁴ And he said, My presence shall go with thee, and I will give thee rest. ¹⁵ And he said unto him, If thy presence go not with me, carry us not up hence. ¹⁶ For wherein shall it be known here that I and thy people have found grace in thy sight? is it not in that thou goest with us? so shall we be separated, I and thy people, from all the people that are upon the face of the earth.

¹⁷ And the LORD said unto Moses, I will do this thing also that thou hast spoken: for thou hast found grace in my sight, and I know thee by name. ¹⁸ And he said, I beseech thee, shew me thy glory. ¹⁹ And he said, I will make all my goodness pass before thee, and I will proclaim the name of the LORD before thee; and will be gracious to whom I will be gracious, and will shew mercy on whom I will shew mercy. ²⁰ And he said, Thou canst not see my face: for there shall no man see me, and live. ²¹ And the LORD said, Behold, there is a place by me, and thou shalt stand upon a rock: ²² And it shall come to pass, while my glory passeth by, that I will put thee in a clift of the rock, and will cover thee with my hand while I pass by: ²³ And I will take away mine hand, and thou shalt see my back parts: but my face shall not be seen.

18.3 God fulfilled Moses' request

Moses asked to see God's glory. He had asked for a very hard thing to be done. Nevertheless, God facilitated his request and made special arrangements for him. This all happened because Moses went hard after God and was not going to take on any new direction until he knew that God was going with him. The Lord was kind to Moses and showed him his back parts (Genesis 32:19-23).

19. Set free from prison

Not many persons want persecutions, but they want the blessings of God. However, those who are called to work for the Lord must expect that they will be persecuted.

19.1 Persecution will follow believers

At many churches, believers will testify that they were doing the work of the Lord and were persecuted. Some of those believers were not expecting to be persecuted, but the Christian life is not free from persecution. Read what Jesus told his disciples will happen to them as they do his work.

Matthew 10:16-25

16 Behold, I send you forth as sheep in the midst of wolves: be ye therefore wise as serpents, and harmless as doves. 17 But beware of men: for they will deliver you up to the councils, and they will scourge you in their synagogues; 18 And ye shall be brought before governors and kings for my sake, for a testimony against them and the Gentiles. 19 But when they deliver you up, take no thought how or what ye shall speak: for it shall be given you in that same hour what ye shall speak. 20 For it is not ye that speak, but the Spirit of your Father which speaketh in you. 21 And the brother shall deliver up the brother to death, and the father the child: and the children shall rise up against their parents, and cause them to be put to death. 22 And ye shall be hated of all men for my name's sake: but he that endureth to the end shall be saved. 23 But when they persecute you in this city, flee ye into another: for verily I say unto you, Ye shall not have gone over the cities of Israel, till the Son of man be come. 24 The disciple is not above his master, nor the servant above his lord. 25 It is enough for the disciple that he be as his master, and the servant as his lord. If they have called the master of the house Beelzebub, how much more shall they call them of his household?

While the disciples suffered persecutions, they were still expecting to continue the work of the Lord. Many persons will think that if they are hurt, then it is time to retreat. However, Jesus reminds believers that they must continue to do his work. To serve the Lord, persons must not give up easily, as Jesus points out to his disciples in Matthew 10:22. Jesus said that he was sending out the disciples as sheep among wolves (Matthew 10:16). From the outset, believers will be attacked, but they must remain wise as serpents. Jesus told the disciples that they will be brought before the council of men (governors and other rulers) for his name's sake.

19.2 God set his children free from prison

As Paul and Silas were working for the Lord, they were persecuted. They cast out a demon from the fortune teller, and her master became angry about Paul's actions, as casting out the demon meant that the owner of the girl would no longer have money from her fortune-telling.

Paul and Silas were reported, and they were placed into prison. However, Paul and Silas sought the same God who had called them into ministry. As they were placed in prison, they sang praise and prayed, and God heard them and delivered them from the prison (Acts 16:25-26). It is seen from reading Acts 16:16-38 that God will defend those who work for him, even if it means destroying a prison to set his children free.

Acts 16:16-40

16 And it came to pass, as we went to prayer, a certain damsel possessed with a spirit of divination met us, which brought her masters much gain by soothsaying: 17 The same followed Paul and us, and cried, saying, These men are the servants of the most high God, which shew unto us the way of salvation. 18 And this did she many days. But Paul, being grieved, turned and said to the spirit, I command thee in the name of Jesus Christ to come out of her. And he came out the same hour.

19 And when her masters saw that the hope of their gains was gone, they caught Paul and Silas, and drew them into the marketplace unto the rulers, 20 And brought them to the magistrates, saying, These men, being Jews, do exceedingly trouble our city, 21 And teach customs, which are not lawful for us to receive, neither to observe, being Romans. 22 And the multitude rose up together against them: and the magistrates rent off their clothes, and commanded to beat them. 23 And when they had laid many stripes upon them, they cast them into prison, charging the jailor to keep them safely: 24 Who, having received such a charge, thrust them into the inner prison, and made their feet fast in the stocks.

25 And at midnight Paul and Silas prayed, and sang praises unto God: and the prisoners heard them. 26 And suddenly there was a great earthquake, so that the foundations of the prison were shaken: and immediately all the doors were opened, and every one's bands were loosed. 27 And the keeper of the prison awaking out of his sleep, and seeing the prison doors open, he drew out his sword, and would have killed himself, supposing that the prisoners had been fled. 28 But Paul cried with a loud voice, saying, Do thyself no harm: for we are all here. 29 Then he called for a light, and sprang in, and came trembling, and fell down before Paul and Silas, 30 And brought them out, and said, Sirs, what must I do to be saved? 31 And they said, Believe on the Lord Jesus Christ, and thou shalt be saved, and thy house.

32 And they spake unto him the word of the Lord, and to all that were in his house. 33 And he took them the same hour of the night, and washed their stripes; and was baptized, he and all his, straightway. 34 And when he had brought them into his house, he set meat before them, and rejoiced, believing in God with all his house. 35 And when it was day, the magistrates sent the serjeants, saying, Let those men go. 36 And the keeper of the prison told this saying to Paul, The magistrates have sent to let you go: now therefore depart, and go in peace. 37 But Paul said unto them, They have beaten us openly uncondemned, being Romans, and have cast us into prison; and now do they thrust us out privily? nay verily; but let them come themselves and fetch us out. 38 And the serjeants told these words unto the magistrates: and they feared, when they heard that they were Romans. 39 And they came and besought them, and brought them out, and desired them to depart out of the city. 40 And they went out of the prison, and entered into the house of Lydia: and when they had seen the brethren, they comforted them, and departed.

Those believers who stand up for God can expect that God will stand up for them. Paul and Silas experienced a God who can deliver his people from prison. They caused the God whom they preached to be seen through their lives. People will often be drawn to the Lord when many believers showcase their God to the world.

The same God who was with Paul and Silas is still available to all believers. As believers put God first in their lives and do that which he has called them to do, they will see God delivering them from many situations. No prison is strong enough to keep a believer who has God working on their behalf. God often provides a way of escape for his children.

20. God blesses those who work for him

Those who are going hard after God may wonder if they will be blessed. It must be known that everyone who works for the Lord will be rewarded. God is a loving and caring God. He lives to reward those who took up his call to work for him.

God will bless his children not just sometimes, but regularly. Therefore, those who are going hard after him can expect that he will bless them daily.

Psalm 68:18-19

18 Thou hast ascended on high, thou hast led captivity captive: thou hast received gifts for men; yea, for the rebellious also, that the LORD God might dwell among them. 19 Blessed be the Lord, who daily loadeth us with benefits, even the God of our salvation. Selah.

God has promised not to withhold anything from those who serve him. Therefore, every believer must be comforted that their hard works for the Lord will be rewarded.

God will give good things to his children as they continue to serve him and do his work. He does not promise to withhold anything, but to freely give those things which are essential for all believers, according to Psalm 84:11.

Psalm 84:10-12

10 For a day in thy courts is better than a thousand. I had rather be a doorkeeper in the house of my God, than to dwell in the tents of wickedness. 11 For the LORD God is a sun and shield: the LORD will give grace and glory: no good thing will he withhold from them that walk uprightly. 12 O LORD of hosts, blessed is the man that trusteth in thee.

20.1 Bringing forth fruit in due season

God wants to plant each believer by the rivers of water. He will cause them to bring forth their fruit in due season. As believers work for him, God will make them blessings to many others. Despite the many challenges that will confront the believers, God will be there to protect them and bless them. Even when the sun beats down on their leaves, God will be there for them and give them victories.

Believers must be aware that when they walk according to God's word, he will be there for them. The blessings which God has for his children will be both invisible and visible, as he loves to bless those who work for him.

Psalm 1:1-3

1 Blessed is the man that walketh not in the counsel of the ungodly, nor standeth in the way of sinners, nor sitteth in the seat of the scornful. 2 But his delight is in the law of the LORD; and in his law doth he meditate day and night. 3 And he shall be like a tree planted by the rivers of water, that bringeth forth his fruit in his season; his leaf also shall not wither; and whatsoever he doeth shall prosper.

God wants to bless all believers so that their lives will be like a tree established by the rivers of water. No amount of heat will cause their leaves to wither. They will bring forth their fruit in the right season.

21. Finish your race strong

There will always be many persons who are preparing for a race. Some of them have the appearance at the beginning that they are the favorite person to win the race, but only one will win in the end. Preparation is one aspect of any sport or examination, but to finish the event is a different thing.

21.1 Keep the faith to the end

Every believer must go hard after God, but they must not become burnt out before the event is completed. Some persons, when they first accept the Lord, are zealous and want to do everything that the Lord has called them to do. However, somewhere along the path in serving the Lord, they become distracted or lose focus. There are many reasons why a believer may drop out of the race. However, God intends not only that all believers zealously start working for the Lord, but that they remain zealous with him until he calls them home to be with them.

2 Timothy 4:7-8

7 I have fought a good fight, I have finished my course, I have kept the faith: 8 Henceforth there is laid up for me a crown of righteousness, which the Lord, the righteous judge, shall give me at that day: and not to me only, but unto all them also that love his appearing.

The Apostle Paul approached the end of his time on earth. As he looked back, he knew that he had not been serving the Lord at an early age. However, when he accepted the Lord on the road of Damascus, he immediately began to preach about the same Jesus whom he persecuted the believers for, according to Acts 9:1-22.

Looking back at his journey, Paul knew that he went hard after God, and that the Lord had to give him many victories. He mentioned that he had fought a good fight (2 Timothy 4:7), which not many believers can say.

When Jesus calls persons to work for him, he wants them to know that they have to fight the battle which is set before them and they must come out victorious. Believers will only be victorious when God is on their side.

The Apostle Paul experienced victories because the Lord was on his side. Because Paul was going hard after God and doing that which the Lord had asked him to do, he was confident that the Lord had laid up a crown of righteousness for him (2 Timothy 4:8).

When a believer starts the race and finishes it according to God's will, then they can be assured that God will reward them greatly.

21.2 Avoid distractions

The Apostle Paul gave some advice to Timothy, one of his spiritual sons. He clearly warned him not to be entangled with the traps which are set before him. There will always be many worldly things, but believers must remain single minded and do that which the Lord has called them to.

2 Timothy 2:1-13

1 Thou therefore, my son, be strong in the grace that is in Christ Jesus. 2 And the things that thou hast heard of me among many witnesses, the same commit thou to faithful men, who shall be able to teach others also. 3 Thou therefore endure hardness, as a good soldier of Jesus Christ. 4 No man that warreth entangleth himself with the affairs of this life; that he may please him who hath chosen him to be a soldier. 5 And if a man also strive for masteries, yet is he not crowned, except he strive lawfully. 6 The husbandman that laboureth must be first partaker of the fruits.

7 Consider what I say; and the Lord give thee understanding in all things. 8 Remember that Jesus Christ of the seed of David was raised from the dead according to my gospel: 9 Wherein I suffer trouble, as an evil doer, even unto bonds; but the word of God is not bound. 10 Therefore I endure all things for the elect's sakes, that they may also obtain the salvation which is in Christ Jesus with eternal glory. 11 It is a faithful saying: For if we be dead with him, we shall also live with him: 12 If we suffer, we shall also reign with him: if we deny him, he also will deny us: 13 If we believe not, yet he abideth faithful: he cannot deny himself.

When believers are going hard after God, they must be aware that there will always be distractions as they pursue him. However, they must know that those stumbling blocks are there to prevent them from fulfilling the will of God.

No believer will experience a life without any stumbling blocks. However, believers must learn how to navigate their ways over and around these stumbling blocks.

Serving Christ takes great courage and requires that believers remain focused on the calling of the Lord upon their lives. To serve the Lord is not easy, but it is rewarding. Many athletes know that their training is never easy. However, their preparation is for a major event. When the day has come, they must be ready for that major event and give it their all. Those who turn back when the race has started cannot expect to be rewarded.

Apostle Paul tells Timothy that a soldier will have to endure difficulty (2 Timothy 2:4). Many believers may not want to experience such challenges, but it comes with the choice to serve the Lord. Believers must continue to go hard after God as they seek to fulfill his calling upon their lives. They are not guaranteed that they will have tomorrow to do the things which they could get done today.

Reference List

Nicholson, F., and Baker, C. (2013). *Certification in risk management assurance.* Altamonte Springs, FL: Institute of Internal Auditors Research Foundation (IIARF).

Shields, J., Brown, M., Kaine, S., Dolle-Samuel, C., North-Samardzic, A., McLean, P., Johns, R., O'Leary, P., Plimmer, G., and Robinson, J. (2016). *Managing employee performance and reward: Concepts, practices, strategies* (2nd ed.). Port Melbourne: Cambridge University Press.

About the Author

The calling of God was evident in the life of Geary Reid at an early age. While he enjoyed his childhood days like all other children, he constantly felt the need to give more attention to God. He eventually surrendered to God in 1986, and his life continues to be used by God.

Geary Reid loves to see God move mightily in the lives of many persons. He does not mind leaving home early in the morning to attend two services on the same day for the Lord. He often attends Bible studies and prayer meetings during the week, because he wants to know more about the God whom he serves. Whenever he preaches, he not only shares the wisdom of God, but also enjoys seeing the manifestation of God among the believers.

Rev. Reid often encourages believers to seek more of God. He likes to see many believers allowing God's spirit to flow through them.

Believers must not see the need to serve the Lord as a part-time commitment. God has been so good to many persons, and he expects that in return, they will acknowledge him and work for him.

Going hard after God is something that every believer ought to do. Life is short and precious, so whatever time is allotted to persons on earth must be meaningful time with the Lord.

Over his years of serving the Lord, Rev. Reid has not seen God blessing lazy people. God is often looking for persons who are diligent to bless them as they do his work. The calling of God upon the lives of every believer is not for personal benefit, but to help other persons to experience the presence and power of God.

Reid is expecting that believers will begin to pick up their mantle and follow God, just as Elisha did. The work of the Lord is great and no one individual can do all of the work, but they must start now and team up with others. Without the help of the Holy Spirit, believers will be exercising much energy, but with little success.

Rev. Reid was asked to preach at Life Changers New Testament Church of God with the theme "Going hard after God." He thanks Pastor Corway Harry for the opportunity to share such an important theme at the church. This church theme has remained in Geary Reid's mind, and he has since penned this literature.

If persons want to be blessed, then going hard after God is one important thing which they can do. Geary Reid has experienced God's blessings, and he works diligently for the Lord. The favor that the Lord has caused to come upon the life of Rev. Reid is tremendous, and he knows that this is partly because he goes hard after God, based on God's calling upon his life.